Feeding Our Souls Within

Inspirational Poetic Words

By

E. Wayne Searles

Copyright © 2017 E. Wayne Searles

All rights reserved.

ISBN-10: 0692905138
ISBN-13: 978-0692905135 (E. Wayne Searles)

DEDICATION

I am dedicating this book of poetry to all of my close friends, family, and to everyone who enjoys reading the poetry I write.

Being a Veteran of the armed forces, I also dedicate my work to all of the men and women who currently serve and who have served! We are all brothers and sisters of another measure!

I would like to honor the following people:

Bernice G. Searles
Mark T. Shelly
Lauren Stephan
Dan Thivierge
Joshua Demarest
Millard "Bud" Linendoll

CONTENTS

	Acknowledgments	i
1	Gone But Not Forgotten	Pg # 1-17
2	Chapter One	Pg # 18-67
3	Chapter Two	Pg # 68-115
4	Chapter Three	Pg # 116-159
5	Chapter Four	Pg # 160-201
6	Chapter Five	Pg # 202-235
7	Chapter Six	Pg # 236-249
8	Biography	Pg # 250

ACKNOWLEDGMENTS

I would like to thank the following people for their contribution of information in order for me to get this book completed.

Rachael Jiles Demarest
Fawn Thivierge
Cody Thivierge
Bambi Thivierge Belon
Donna Lourie
Janette Shelly
Maegen Shelly
Abraham Shelly
Paul Stephan
Kimberly Cole Epstein
Brenda Searles Ebert

A very special thanks to my son **Thomas Wayne Searles** for helping me and listening to me and showing interest in my writing. Thomas is my sound board and has been a great help with editing this book. Thank you son!

Many thanks to the readers who read my poetry and support me. Many thanks to **Sydney Linendoll,** who loves reading my poetry and is always asking when I will publish another book. Your appreciation of my poetry is a great motivation, it helps me to keep on going, thank you.

GONE BUT NOT FORGOTTEN

Millard "Bud" Linendoll
27 July 1957 To 4 May 2017

"May you rest in peace Bud"

E. Wayne Searles

Dear Departed Mother

Each passing day
tears form and roll down my face
All I have now
are memories of my mother to embrace

Every time I look at a photo
I see her wonderful smile
It's hard to believe she is gone
Just trying to believe it's just for a short while

Hard to grasp such thoughts
that she has been buried in the earth
I truly miss this woman
the woman I called mother and who gave me birth

We had such a bond
she protected me any way she could
My mother was a woman
who did nothing but good

Dear mother
your smile I still see every day
I am happy you no longer suffer
but I am so sad you had to go away

Mom I truly love you
my heart is broken in so many ways
Every time I go outside
I think of you when in the sky I gaze

My heart will eventually heal
I will laugh and smile when thinking of you
I will never ever forget your legacy
to the heavens I promise this to you

Feeding Our Souls Within

BERNICE G. SEARLES
My Mother
22 Feb 1928 to 27 Sept 2015

"May you rest in peace Mother"

E. Wayne Searles

My Dear Friend Mark

I am so lost for words
I lost a brother yesterday
Not a brother by blood
but a brother in a best friend kind of way

The news was so sudden
unexpected in every way
Today I find myself lost
searching for so many words to say

Mark, my brother
a very dear friend you were to me
I can't believe you're gone
I can't fathom this reality

My sincere condolences to your family
as I am thinking of you all, so very hard today
It is an unbearable pain to lose you
leaving many with no words to say

You were a mentor
loving husband and father, it's true
You were very successful
with everything that you would do

I sit here my dear friend
I ponder all the reasons why
Your loss brings me tears
we never had a chance to even say goodbye

Just know I love you my brother
I love your family too
Rest in peace in the heavens
where God is now watching over you

Mark T. Shelly
29 Sept 1959 to 27 Sept 2016

"May you rest in peace Mark"

E. Wayne Searles

Beloved Lauren

Long blonde hair
as beautiful as can be
A joy to everyone's heart
a girl of pure serenity

So much love to offer
with a family bond so very tight
The kind of bond where you would say I love you
before saying good night

Our beloved Lauren
our lives were so blessed with you
In our eyes you could do no wrong
because our bond was true

So many great times we shared
so many memories made
We will never forget you
our memories will never ever fade

The good Lord has taken you
for what reasons we just don't know
we only wish we had a last goodbye
before you had to go

We know you are in heaven
as an angel that you are
We understand you have left us
but haven't gone so very far

We feel your loving spirit
every single day
We just wish it wasn't true
that you have forever gone away

Lauren J. Stephan
24 June 1997 to 23 May 2016

"May you rest in peace Lauren"

E. Wayne Searles

Today I Left You

Today I left you
as you stood at my bedside to say goodbye
I wish I didn't have to go
but we know the reasons why

Now I am in a place
where pain is no more
I am watching over each of you
you're my loving children whom I adore

Please don't be angry
try to lift the burden that brings you tears
Keep all of our loving memories
of everything we did through the years

I may be gone
but within each of you I still live
Take care of my grand children
as you all have so much love to give

I am watching you right now
I know you hurt so bad
Just know I love you so much
I am your loving dad

I know you're going to miss me
I will miss you too
I will never say goodbye
because my spirit will always be with you

So please smile
and think happy thoughts for me
I will be right here waiting
when someday heaven is your place to be

Daniel E. Thivierge
29 Dec 1963 to 17 Feb 2016

"May you rest in peace Dan"

"DEDICATED TO JOSHUA DEMAREST"

So Young

So young
but the good Lord took him away
There must be another plan for his spirit
God does work in a mysterious way

Young, active, and full of joy
Joshua has been taken from this world today
To everyone who knew Joshua
please don't let his memories fade away

Tragic and so very sad
in every imaginable way
I kneel before you today oh Lord
and for Joshua's family I pray and pray

The pain and grief that endures us
when we someone so precious to the heart
It leaves us with an empty feeling
not knowing how to realize from us they did depart

Time they say heals
but that time usually goes by very slow
It is at this time
you can count on all friends and family you should know

May God be with you all
in these days which we mourn
Let us all find fond memories of Joshua
allowing healing to all hearts that have been torn

So Young
Continued

In Gods precious name
we pray that Joshua is in your arms today
As we all try to understand dear Lord
any reasons why you took him away

Written: 15 December 2016

Joshua J. Demarest
15 June 2003 to 13 Dec 2016

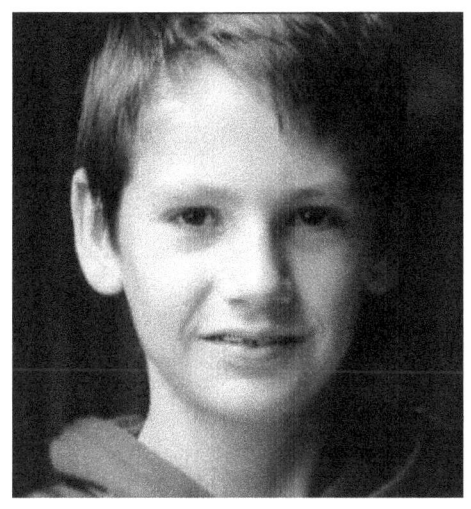

"May you rest in peace Joshua"

By Rachael Jiles Demarest:
Joshua is my third child but he was my first born son. It was through him that I learned how truly strong and special a mother and son bond can be. As a baby and toddler we were inseparable. Even as a thirteen year old, he would still give me a kiss before he would go anywhere. He was a sweet young man who loved sports, playing outside and hanging with friends. He loved to make people laugh and his smile really could light up a room. I miss his smile and his laugh. Every day without him is hard, but every day he is remembered and every day he is loved.

By E. Wayne Searles:
To all of the families and loved ones of these people I have dedicated poetry to in this book. My heart goes out to each and every one of you. The death of a loved one is never easy!

In our daily lives we get so busy and side tracked, forgetting the little things and the most important things in life. We tend to forget to say I love you, or to forgive, after being angry with each other. Time on this earth is really very short and we need to make the best of it. We need to make as many lasting memories as we can and enjoy this journey through life that we have been blessed to have.

We all lose loved ones along the way, in this life we live. These times are hard, but we get through them and we move on. It does not mean we have to forget the people we lose from our lives, it only means that there comes a time when we accept it and keep all the good memories of them to think about.

In this past year I have dear friends that have lost a husband, a father, a child and I lost my dear mother. I wanted to take the time to recognize these people that we have lost as they were awesome people that will never be forgotten. My sincere condolences to my dear friends and the families of those that have passed on.

By no means am I exploiting anyone to make profit with this book. The dedications are sincere, they are to show the families that I care and that their loved ones will never be forgotten!

Joshua, I did not personally know, but he is from my home town area where people are close for the most part and when times get hard, everyone will help each other, that, you can count on! I feel that I am still part of that community and share my feelings for his loss.

Mark was a dear friend and mentor. I would visit Mark and his family on various weekends and sit outside and have great conversation with Mark about web pages and just life in general. I have had many friends over the years and from many places around the world, but the loss of my friend Mark was very hard for me. I certainly miss Mark and his greeting me when I would go visit him. He would always shake my hand and say "Hey man" He left behind a very loving and dear family whom are and always will be family to me. I met Mark and his family in 2009 in the Czech Republic. A wonderful family whom I think of as my family. I have traveled around the western side of the world and have made many friends, but the Shelly's hold a place dearest to my heart! When Mark left us, I lost the best friend I have ever had! Mark was a man that was wanting to help people and he had so many great idea's. Mark had a vision and was certainly the kind of people we need more of in this world. Mark, I sure miss you brother! We will drink tea in heaven again one day. R.I.P. Brother!!! You are missed dearly! To the Shelly family, my sincere condolences to you. I love you guys to the moon and back!

Lauren, I knew, as she is the daughter of my dear friends Paul and Kimberly. The good Lord took another angel to the heavens the day he took Lauren! I remember Lauren getting her learners permit and driving her mother around. Lauren had great parents and family members. She was brought up quite well and was a wonderful young lady. She will be missed by all and remain in the hearts of us all. My heart sincerely goes out to Paul and Kim for this

Dan, is the father of dear friends of mine, whom are like family to me. I have met Dan, but did not really know him on a personal level. He was a loving father and a hard worker. Dan is missed by so many and was loved by so many. He touched the hearts of so many. Knowing Dan's children is enough to allow me to know he was a good man and a gentle giant. My heart goes out to the Thivierge families for their loss as I know it has been very hard for them. My sincere condolences to all of you, Cody, Bambi, and Fawn. I love you guys! May your loving dad Rest In Peace!

My mother, oh how I miss her every single day. So many memories made, but I wish I could turn back the hands of time and change the tides. My mother was a Morehouse and came from a big family. My mom passed on 27 September 2015, exactly one year to the day that my friend Mark passed! My dear mother, Bernice, was a great woman and loved by many. I was not able to attend her services, but she knows I loved her and therefore I dedicate my poetry to a women who taught me well and loved me so!

In 2015, my son Thomas Wayne Searles and I made a trip from Europe to visit friends and family and so he could visit his grandmother. We knew she was ill and not doing very well. It was the last time Thomas was able to see and spend time with his grandmother. It about brings me to tears to write this, as we miss her so. My mom was in a lot of pain and it helped me to accept her passing. I know for sure she is in Heaven watching over us all and spending all the time she can with the spirits of her siblings there.

Calling My Name II

Calling my name
like I've heard a thousand times before
Little did I know
it was the last time he would walk out that door

Never even thinking
it was the last time to say goodbye
Never even thinking
he would never again say hi

Still calling my name
is what I hear in my mind
Turning around to look
nobody behind the voice to find

Tears build up
as I realize he is gone
I look out the window
and see him standing on the lawn

The pain sets in
as I realize the voice will fade away
He has gone to heaven
and there he will have to stay

Dear Lord you have taken him
my heart broken and torn in two
I know it was not in anger
it was what you had to do

E. Wayne Searles

Calling My Name II
Continued

We really love and miss him
wanting him back to love and cherish
Our son, such a loving soul
we had no idea he was about to perish

To my dear son
with all the love from my heart
Your memory will always be with me
even though this world you had to part

This poem is dedicated to all of you who have lost a loved one and find it hard to let them go. Sometimes we still feel them around or see them around, even though they are forever gone.

This concludes the dedication section of this poetry book. If you have received this book as a gift or you have purchased my book, thank you for reading my poetry. Thank you for taking the time out of your life to read the words I write. You may find that some of my poems can be very deep or some of them might seem confusing or some may just seem sad or emotional. Please know that I write in a way that my poetry can touch the souls of everyone and everyone is different. Some poems are about personal experiences and others are based on how I believe other people feel.

Thanks again for taking the time and choosing my poetry book.

Sincerely,
Author: E. Wayne Searles

Chapter One

Blind Emotion

From stirred up emotions
blindly I shed a tear
It comes from something I saw
something very emotional or dear

Every day I live this life
trying to understand how it's suppose to be
I find that I have an emotional soul
always setting my tears free

Some things are so terrible
and so sad it's hard to see
How some people's lives are distraught
and a daily part of reality

If the world weren't so harsh
because people become so self centered every day
True emotion could help to cleanse
taking such brutal actions away

A true emotional mindset
will share your true humanity
Stop worrying what others think
allow yourself to be free, emotionally

Without any given notice
is why blindly, is what I say
It can be from happiness or sadness
it's just a cleansing from tear drops under way

E. Wayne Searles

911
The Fall Of The Towers

Eleven September 2001
fifteen years ago you see
Terrorist performed a horrible act
that brought America down on one knee

So many people perished
never knowing what their fate was going to be
I cannot imagine their horror
or their last minutes and every plea

The truth may never be known
of what really happened on that day
I remember how I felt
having absolutely no words to say

Time has moved forward
to forget 911 we never will
The memory will not evade us
forever leaving us with a terrible chill

Very, very, painful
dear God watch over all, who are still in so much pain
Find a way to give the survivors peace
so not to live a life in vain

911
Continued

Although this day was so very tragic
it brought the American people together on that day
Brothers and sisters undivided
for this, there aren't many words to say

Let's forget the conspiracy theories
or the hatred, from this we tend to feel
Let's focus for a moment on the victims
and all the families that still need to heal

"May all the 911 victims rest in peace"
"Gone, but not forgotten"

A Point Of View

What is it you want to read?
why is it I can't write about rainbows and sunny skies?
Why is it people fight so much
and everyone always telling lies

Everyone has a painted picture
of the way they want life to be
Full of rainbows and sunny skies
no more hatred amongst all of humanity

That would be very special
but problems there still would be
People have been fighting since the beginning of time
it's just pure reality

Nothing should be set in stone
we should be able to get along
Everyone needs to participate
and be forgiven when we are wrong

There should be no elite
equality is certainly the best way to go
Life would be so much better
wouldn't you say it's so?

I paint pictures in my mind too
but they are of reality
I try to share them with you all
even if it's not what you want to see

A Point Of View
Continued

I have a view point
with just about everything I write
So wrap your thoughts around this poem
and now it's time to say good night

E. Wayne Searles

All Lives Matter

It's about humanity
and being equally the same
It's about all lives matter
something we all should claim

It all needs to stop
the fighting and segregation needs to end
Love and peace for all humanity
is the message we all should send

Black lives matter
hugs for free, says it in a very special way
We all need to stop killing each other
something that is happening every single day

It's time to call a truce
and hug each other today
Let the police serve and protect
and everyone just put their guns away

This is our time
time to teach the young a much better way
To teach them more about love and peace
bringing America back together again I say

Whether you're red, yellow, black, or white
we all bleed the same
So to everyone I say
all lives matter should be our official claim

All Lives Matter
Continued

To all of my brothers and sisters
lets stand together for peace and love
Let's make our world a better place to live
and prays thanks to the great God above

E. Wayne Searles

Blind Sacrifice

You don't have a clue
you have no idea how I truly feel
You're all about your selfish ways
the rest of the days of my life you steal

Caught up in a world of your own
thinking everything is normal as can be
I am here to say it isn't
I almost want to set myself free

Your blind ambitions help you
and I am paying a hefty price
You are too blind to see it
for me it's an ultimate sacrifice

Every day for me it gets worse
because so fast the time goes by
Every day I find myself in a state of confusion
asking myself over and over, why

I know my reasons
but I am now seeing your reasons too
There is so much emptiness between us
oh God what should I do

If I were to leave you tomorrow
you would be upset and cry
You would try breaking your barriers of blindness
asking yourself over and over, why

Blind Sacrifice
Continued

My state of confusion is becoming reality
I'm tired of thinking about it every day
It's getting to a point of decision
I'm almost ready to finally walk away

E. Wayne Searles

Escaping The Fingers Of Death

Slipping from the fingers of death
I once again grasp a fresh breath of air
Some of my choices in life are chaotic
I make it like this with no despair

Always feeling like a goner
at times it's even hard to catch my breath
Feeling so closed in
I only focus and worry about my death

Such depression is alive
a feeling of denial with much grief
Always watching and waiting for the reaper
to come take me away like a thief

Immortal souls swim
in a world beyond what we call reality
They often reach out and touch us
trying to show us what they see

My energy is diminished
by the touching of souls from the other side
This can be very depressing
makes me want to run and hide

I may often break free
from the grasp that reaches through deaths door
I try to break from this depression
searching for my energy to restore

Escaping The Fingers Of Death
Continued

This life is but once
please let me live it well
I do not wish to go with you
my soul I do not wish to sell

I Really Love life

I really love life
but something seems to be broken inside
Maybe that's why I think so much
and my feelings I try to hide

Life to me has so much meaning
it's great to open my eyes each and every day
It's a wonderful feeling to live
and be happy I have done my best in every possible way

It would be a lie if I were to say
that I am afraid to die
I would not be here with my friends
to wish myself a farewell goodbye

I don't really know what is broken
I just know something doesn't feel quite right
I just know life is so precious
and the dreams I have are so far out of sight

I realize now
I have to live with whatever has come my way
I am happy with many things I have
but somehow lost for many words to say

Relaxation and contemplation
I seek an answer to the hands of time to find
They tick so slow, but yet so fast
allowing this wonderful life to unwind

I Really Love Life
Continued

Maybe nothing is broken
and everything is the way it's supposed to be
Maybe the feelings I'm having
are just feelings I really need to set free

E. Wayne Searles

Lake Of Tears

It was in my early years
I was betrayed by the likes of me
I allowed myself to be treated badly
finding a way out, I couldn't see

Only wanting to fit in
to enjoy the same things as everyone around
Only I was not to be heard
my voice did not have a sound

Whenever others didn't have a friend around
on any given day
Then they were my friend
but it's not something they would really like to say

I lived in silence
for most of my life, I can recall
I was used and abused
mentally absorbing it all

There is an imaginary lake
from all the tears I cried throughout the years
Now it's only memories I have
I did away with all the fears

Eventually I changed my path
the one I walked was lonely and too sharp for my feet
I eventually broke my silence
self betrayal had to be beat

Lake Of Tears
Continued

I may have come a long ways in life
but my memories take me to that lake every day
I thank God I have been strong
for I did not take my life away

E. Wayne Searles

Life Thereafter

Hello, where am I
it's awful dark in here
Why can't I see
it's dark, but I have no fear

Is that shadows
or figures that I'm starting to see
Why is it they are so sad
do they not see me

My pain is gone
that is not normal for me
Something seems so different
I feel totally free

Oh no, who are all of these other people
no, this cannot be so
I have heard so many stories
but was always afraid to go

I wasted so many years
being afraid to die
Now I know why I'm in darkness
just not sure if I heard everyone say goodbye

Look at all those lights now
it's no longer dark and I can see
Oh my God, there is life after death
they are so happy to see me

Life Thereafter
Continued

Dear family
please don't worry or be so sad
I may no longer walk with you
but where I am is not all that bad

I am thankful
that my beliefs were right
Because he was at the gate waiting
he made me an angel to watch over you all each night

Lonely Inspiration

Inspired by the road
driving lonely through the night
The only thing I see
is what my lights put in sight.

So many thoughts
are running through my head
Wondering if I were not here
where would I be instead

I travel along a path
not sure if it was chosen or meant to be
Only knowing feelings of being unhappy
this can't be right for me

Not sure if it's the road or the music
or traveling alone in this car
I only keep thinking
true happiness can't be far

It is a shame
a married man should feel so, so alone
His car is his best friend
many places to him are shown

This is a time for thinking
about all actions of which to take
Trying to overcome loneliness
and see through people who are fake

Lonely Inspiration
Continued

Tonight, this distance
that I drive in my car
Allows me to think
in this life I've come pretty far

Times of being alone can heal
a bad moment from your day
When all you do is think
and have no words to say

Inspired by the road
clearing all thoughts on which I thrive
This part of my path was destined
even if it is a lonely drive

I sort my thoughts
weighing the cons and the pros
Dealing with what I have in life
sometimes that is the way it goes

I am what I am
needing to be cared for and loved as a friend
I may be lonely
but will be happy in the end

I like my lonely drives
especially during the night
It helps me to see
many things not shown by any light

E. Wayne Searles

Lonely

Why do I feel the way I do
why do I feel the way I feel
I feel like a machine
a machine with a broken seal

My mind keeps turning and turning
I wonder what my future holds for me
As I look around
I am taking in everything I see

Slow motion is the picture
thoughts never end
Some sort of broken feeling
something I am trying to mend

Unhappy is the moment
unhappy is how I live
I gave everything
I feel I have nothing more to give

Holding onto a threshold
where I know there is much meaning to life
The one who makes me so unhappy
I would have to say is my wife

In the beginning I really loved her
somehow those feeling have all been flushed away
Now I find myself in the moment
living day by day

Lonely
Continued

The feeling of a broken heart
tears fill my soul
Moving though this world of slow motion
searching for a goal

I hope happiness finds me
as I'm lurking across this land
Waiting for that special someone
to come and grab my hand

When true happiness finds me
these bad feelings will go away
I will have found that special someone
to be by my side every day

All of these emotions
controlling how I feel
At one time you all have been there
I am sure you know the deal

Yes I'm sad and lonely
and feeling very bad
I know better days will come
better than what I've had

E. Wayne Searles

Mental State

My mental state
revolves from the likes of me
It is created
from everything I hear and see

People seem to have their thoughts
wondering who I am
That doesn't matter at all
I really don't give a damn

What is most certain
are the thoughts of me
Whether I live in illusion
or in my very own reality

Everyone is so very different
but in many cases so much the very same
People notice your actions
because they know the rules of the game

No I am not crazy
my mind just works a different way
It seeks out clarification
of everything others do or say

My, self analysis
creates my very own mental state
It's what makes us different
but allows us to somehow relate

Mental State
Continued

So never judge me
as I do not judge you
We are all very special
within everything we say or do

E. Wayne Searles

Message To Self

To my beloved self
I can love you so others can too
You must learn right from wrong
as everyone will see through you

Be nice to others
and they will be the same to you
Maybe not everyone
and you can't force them to

Find thanks within
as you've been given a blessing to live
Take from the things you learn
offering knowledge to give

I am your mentor
this whole life through
I am here to help you turn the page
I will show you a broader view

There will be times of confusion
as well as sadness, depression, and feeling all alone
Together we will get through it
because it's just emotions, it's not set in stone

You are very precious
to yourself and everyone in some special way
Be proud of the life you live
be thankful for what you have every day

Selling Out Your Soul

Beneath your flesh
lies a soul dark to the core
It is in defiance
you have no idea what's in store

You feed it a passion of anger
from your regrets and remorse that you bestow
This dark soul is ready for vengeance
say it isn't so

On a reckless path
from a journey chosen by you
Your time of no longer being in control is near
there is nothing you can do

You smoke and drink
cussing words from a vial mouth of hate and misery
Your visions of life are drenched
with a lethal solution, you can't be set free

No acknowledgement of your loss
you're determined what you do is right
You are very cold to the bones
you have no sense of inner sight

The creator of your destiny
you create your very own path to hell
A very dark soul inside of you is taking over
to an evil world your soul you did sell

E. Wayne Searles

Monster In The Mirror

Are you my family
are we related but have no ties
Are you a family member
that is rebellious and so evil, also full of lies

Why must you inflict pain
onto a family member like me
Life is too short
to always have such negativity

Find peace
within your own soul
Stop being so negative
before it takes its final toll

Family should be precious
to love each other and not fight
It's time to stop the negativity and hate
it's time to do what's right

If you're my family
a brother or sister or another relation
We should stick together
there should be no contemplation

If you're blood related
and want nothing to do with me
Just fade away
you and your negativity!

Monster In The Mirror
Continued

No love is a loss
sorry about how you may feel
Loving the family you have is important
nothing could be more real

Unfortunately the hurt can't be hidden
from the damage you try to do
There is a monster looking at you in the mirror
and no realization sinks in, that the monster is you

E. Wayne Searles

My Rival / My Friend

You are my rival
you try to make me think you are my friend
You will say anything
you are a master of pretend

I am not your enemy
I am not your rival in my mind
I don't play pretend
it's just not how I am defined

I am very honest
I truly say it, like it is to say
I speak many words needing spoken
I don't keep any of them at bay

I don't know how others define you
or how you have been treated, to make you this way
You should just be up front
whenever you have something you really want to say

To bury your feelings of need
with a façade that only you believe
Honest love and friendship is hard to find
it's something you cannot conceive

We may not be on the same terms
everyone has a path to follow to an end
Maybe it's time you break down your barriers
accept love and understanding from a true friend

My Rival / My Friend
Continued

This is your path in life
it is your terms in which you choose to live
No more need to be a rival
here is my hand, an offer of peace I give

E. Wayne Searles

My Words – My Medicine

Very deep
below several layers are the words I write
They are from buried emotion
they are someone's internal fight

Many people quiver
from stained emotions left deep inside
Not knowing how to release them
they only know how to hide

My words are like a medicine
I try to grasp what you fail to see
I try to help you see within
and bring you back to reality

Living our lives
we sometimes forget who we really are
We bury hurt so deep
it drags behind us and we don't get very far

So I am a poet
it's my choice and my passion
I try to write such deep words
in a mind gripping fashion

My heart is strong
filled with so much love that's pure
I pray my words dig deep
and help your emotions to be more secure

My Words / My Medicine
Continued

Don't allow your thoughts to lead you blind
thinking reality is the way we live every day
Set yourself free from constant thoughts
may my words be your medicine in such a way

Silence

Silence
is no longer the realm of my mind
I am just stir crazy
no inner peace of any kind

Something certainly invades me
constant thinking of what to do
My nerves are on edge
trying not to believe what is really true

Something is about to hit me really hard
I feel the energy of it all
I am in shambles
as if I am about to fall

Am I strong
like I use to once be
Can I take
everything that is happening to me

Perhaps this is a turning point
in a direction my life has to go
Change is inevitable
this I can tell you so

As I break these barriers
from where I was before
My next step in life
will be through a wide open door

Silence
Continued

Things may have turned me upside down
and caused some chaos for me
I will handle it all in stride
it won't bring me to a knee

… E. Wayne Searles

Taking Your Life

By: E. Wayne Searles

You want to leave this world
because you can't take the pain
You allow the words of others
to drive you madly insane

Not knowing which way to turn
voices grow louder in your head
They scream louder than your conscience
telling you, you're better off dead

You cry from inside
and you cry out to the world in which you live
You tell yourself it isn't so
but if asked, your hand you would give

The demons take you over
you feel as if you can no longer catch your breath
Your world is crashing in
and the answer to you is only death

So caught up in misguided thought
not giving you a chance to think clear
You think of taking your life away
without any sense of fear

Life can be very bad
having times that we truly hate
To change your thoughts of dying
gives you a chance to change your fate

Taking Your Life
Continued

Take a deep breath
try to think in a positive way
Don't take that unforgiving step
I beg of you with these words I say

E. Wayne Searles

Tear Drops

Understanding another person
as tears roll down their cheek
Getting a touch of emotion
from a situation that seems so bleak

Some people cry from happiness
some people cry from sad moments that they feel
Allowing themselves to cry at all
is a moment, they allow themselves to heal

Tear drops are very heavy
as gravity pulls them to the ground
Full of cleansed emotion
they splash without a sound

Breaking a smile on their face
relieved from feelings they once had
It seems the tear drops I saw
where from that person being sad

Reaching out my hand
to console this person, in moments need
A silent word is spoken
I offer my help with understanding and not an ounce of greed

Allowing myself to understand
someone's feelings from teardrops that I see
I know they would do the same
if teardrops were cleansing me

This Place I hate

I cannot breathe
the stench of bodies is in the air
They just keep piling us in
they don't really seem to care

An institution of care
but a business with only money on the mind
They feed us medication
to try to keep us blind

I keep my wits about me
during these moments of building anxiety
To others there is absolutely nothing wrong
but they just can't see what I can see

I was told to close my eyes
but that's a world where no one wants to go
If you want to hear my story
I will certainly tell you so

At times, I hate this life I live
often I keep in everything how I feel
At times it's just so confusing
I am sure many others know the deal

E. Wayne Searles

This Life

Why is it we all have to eventually die
why life can't be forever, I say
We work so hard to make it nice
then we leave everything behind and just go away

Somehow it doesn't seem fair
and many times I just wish it wasn't so
We start out as a baby
then end up like a baby before we go

We create so many moments
make so many friends along the way
We go about our lives
each and every day

We don't always realize
or contemplate what it all is for
Time goes by so fast
we get old and realize how much, life we do adore

Could you imagine being immortal
not aging in life or worrying we will die
We could continue on our wayward journey
life would be great I don't deny

But then again we get tired
pain and suffering takes its toll
So eventually dying isn't really so bad
being it is our last and final role

This Life
Continued

Some of us fear death
some of us, death we do not fear
It's just a circle of life
and a time for the living to shed a tear

This world is just a beginning
our next world we will have so much more
So when it's our time to go
have no fear when you stand at the open door

E. Wayne Searles

Thoughts This Path Brought Me To

Sitting here, I wonder
about the path I have chosen
Thoughts seem a bit blurry
and are a bit frozen

It seems like destiny
has a fate for me unknown
For this path I have chosen
Is leaving me feeling so alone

Even though this is my feeling
I have 3 kids to love me so
They only know that I'm their daddy
and they need my returning love to make them glow

There is such a negative charge
pushing down on my soul
It seems to be this place I'm in
feeling like I can't go

I am at a point
where the pressure is too great
I feel the need to travel
to seek my true fate

A Sagittarius I am
born under the sign of the sun
I only want to travel
away from my family I will not run

Thought This Path Brought Me To
Continued

When life gets to a point
where a person has to wonder who they are
It is truly a time to evaluate
the path they have traveled thus far

I know I have an absence
my mind tells me so
On the 14th of July
It will be time to go

I will return
when my freedom allows me to
I love you all
and promise to come back to you

E. Wayne Searles

Tired With Blind Fate

Sometimes I just want to say goodbye
tired of everything I do or see
Tired of being bound in chains
not even able to be me

Sometimes I can't control the hate
a feeling burning deep inside
There are times when I lose it
it's one hell of a ride

I am in a place now
where I don't really want to be
Everything around me causes pain
how can I release it all from me

Normal days and days of sorrow
seem almost the same
I just don't know how to change it
therefore I hold myself to blame

Dysfunctional in every manor
nothing goes right
I would love to end it all
but something makes me fight

How much more strength do I have
for this façade of a life I live
So tired of being a helper
having nothing left to give

Tired With Blind Fate
Continued

Chaos is the name
wanting or not wanting to die
Confusion blinds my ambitions
making me feel like I want to say goodbye

E. Wayne Searles

When I Close My Eyes Today

I close my eyes and see
bright lights in an empty space
I think of my father
wanting to see his face

I never knew I could miss him
we grew apart many years ago
I wish things could have been different
this I now know

I built up certain hatred
it burned deep within
I didn't get a last goodbye
I live with my very own sin

Why did you just let your little boy go
letting him feel no love from you
All he needed was a father
but it's something that wasn't for you

Now I am a father
I have boys of my own
I show them love every day
so they will not hate me when they are grown

Now they need me like I needed you
I don't know why you pushed me away
It has been ten years you've been gone
but I find myself missing you today

When I Close My Eyes Today
Continued

Sleep well dear father
some day we will meet on the other side
In the meantime I have a family to love
and a few more years on this roller coaster of life to ride

E. Wayne Searles

Worth The Keep

You ever just get so tired
of certain things in this life
They cause you to find yourself
looking down the barrel of a gun or at a blade of a knife

Often you ask yourself why
and what is your reason to be
At this point in your life
some things you clearly cannot see

You should just stop what you're doing
and take another look around
Things in your life can change
things that you love can be found

Giving yourself another chance
opening your eyes to see another day
Only to find
all the bad things have mysteriously gone away

Wanting to live
having a will for what can be
This alone my friend
will again allow you to see

Find strength deep
bring out the best in you
The tiresome feeling will vanish
giving you happiness again to pursue

Worth The Keep
Continued

So think of my words as a weapon
let them pierce you deep
Put down that gun or knife
your life is worth the keep

E. Wayne Searles

Yesterday's Gone

Today
is so different than any day of our past
Our futures are of chaos
borders being over taken very fast

Europe undergoing change
a change that leaves the country weak
So many refugees coming from the east
they say it's food and shelter that they seek

America being torn apart
mostly from within, is what I see
Our government so very greedy
always telling lies to you and me

Everyone sick and tired
but no one wants to stand and fight
Politicians get their votes
the people hope their choices were right

There just seems to be no end
to the corruption and crime today
All of the countries are poisoned
and we just listen to what the government leaders say

What if everyone finally took a stand
to change the way things have turned out to be
To stop the movement of refugees
and to stop terrorist mobility

Yesterday's Gone
Continued

To everyone I say
stand up for what you do believe
Be united together in good
but not in a way in which you will deceive

Chapter Two

Seemingly Angry

Just when I seem angry
you have no idea what's going on in my head
You have no idea who I am
or why I have said what I've said

I am in a transition
between good and bad
I am trying to have a better life
better than what I've had

Trying to find an understanding
of what it is that makes me tick
I am finding that ignorance of others
tends to make me sick

Roaming around this world
trying to figure out my plan
Trying to give it my best
I'll do all that I can

So I seem a little angry
just give me my space
Give me a little time
to wipe this angry look off my face

I know it's not the end of the world
as anger comes and goes
I'm sorry you had to see it
I'm sorry that it shows

E. Wayne Searles

Dreams Are Our Reality

What if our shadows were real
and we were just a vision of its mind
It sounds a bit bizarre
I think you all will find

What if this life
is just an image in someone's dream
Where everything we do
is not as it may seem

What if when I sleep
my dreams are a reality that's real
Then when I am awake
there is no reality to grasp or feel

A misguided illusion
like, is the earth flat or round
When we are awake we can hear
but when we dream, we don't hear a sound

Have I lost you yet
with such confusing or ironic words I write
When you say good morning
do you really mean good night

Imagine your dreams as reality
and your daily life not real at all
When do we finally wake up
is it when we get our final call

Dreams Are Our Reality
Continued

Life after death
there is life on the other side
It's when we wake up from this dream
our shadows become reality and our bodies made to hide

Either buried or burnt
the dream finally over as we awake
It's time to move on
from this life that has always been fake

E. Wayne Searles

Feeling lost

Feeling lost
is sometimes how we feel
Having moments in life
that are so very real

Feeling very confused
so distant from everything around
Being able to hear
but ignore every sound

So many things on our mind
that put us in a daze
As we daydream about our problems
just a passing faze

At times it's a lonely feeling
when we feel like we're stuck
Always trying to figure out
how to earn that extra buck

Life throws us obstacles
it's up to us to figure everything out
Sometimes this can be so difficult
that is without a doubt

When you're in a faze like this
please do not despair
Everything will work out somehow
this message I wanted to share

I too have moments
when life just seems so down
I have come to realize
it's no reason to have a frown

Feeling Lost
Continued

Everything happens for a reason
along this path we walk
When you're feeling lonely
find a friend with whom you can talk

E. Wayne Searles

I Am Fearful

I see a blizzard
as I look into the night, starry sky
Many thoughts of the day
so many questions that ask why

In fear of our future
because of the way things are
Not sure if I will find the answers
by looking in the sky at some bright star

So here I am, just a man
the puppet master pulls my strings too
I fight this battle with nothing to gain
hoping for a better future, it's what I do

The stars are pretty
I'm thankful for them to be able to see
I may be a puppet like you all
but at least I am me

Our fate is in blueprint
it's just something we cannot see
The world around us is changing
so very rapidly

Times of change are needed
it's not something that the stars do tell
Hatred of mankind has gone wild
living on earth these days, is like living in hell

I Am Fearful
Continued

We need to start trusting one another
giving a helping hand when someone is in need
We shouldn't turn our heads and walk away
when someone will just lay there and bleed

E. Wayne Searles

I Am Very Tired

You read what I write
you hear my words I silently speak
Troubling times have me bewildered
feeling like I am at my breaking peak

I keep on thinking
everything will eventually be okay
Those are the thoughts
that get me through each and every day

Trying to be strong
seemingly happy, when you look at my face
Enduring the pressure from both sides
realizing it's time to embrace

My views of this world
slowly changing the way I feel
Nothing going right
not an ounce of positive energy to steal

I am very tired
feelings overwhelm with desire to flee
I gave all of my love away
don't have even enough left to love me

No tear drops to fall
I am empty as a dried out well
No heart inside
because of lack of love my heart fell

I Am Very Tired
Continued

My voice is ever so silent
but you know I am here
I write all these words
because I can't shed a tear

Why is it this way
everything has to be
Only wanting to be happy
but now from all of this wanting to be free

No more love or tears
my feelings are getting very cold
This man in this body
so hurt and confused growing lonely and old

E. Wayne Searles

I better Not Unwind

I'm just about one second
from a secret that resides in me
At a point of destruction
something nobody else can see

I left my place of frustration
looked for a place to go
My demons are fighting me
this, I tell you so

I found a place for a drink
a little Jack Daniels, to relax the other side of me
I sit and sip my drink
offering hope for the powers to be

All around me is chaos
not a choice made by me
I am so tired of this shit
I ask myself, what is reality

There is another soul
amidst the realm in which I live
It loves to anger me
into the purity of alcohol, myself I give

I ask nobody for help
whatever happens is what is meant to be
I shall play Russian roulette with my decisions
I let my inhibitions control the likes of me

I Better Not Unwind
Continued

I have an angry soul
no true happiness to be found
I am an emotional wound up tension
that's about to be unwound

E. Wayne Searles

I Feel Like A Mouse

I'll just scurry to my corner
because I feel like a mouse
I am lost in lust and confusion
after losing my recent spouse

I sit here all day
thoughts constantly going through my mind
No matter how much I examine them
the more I feel like a mouse, I find

What has cause such chaos
to get me off track and lose
Why can't I just wake up
and stop drinking all this booze

Frightened I am
of what will be my uncertain fate
I loved my wife dearly
it's not knowing what happened, that I hate

So to my small corner I will scurry
just to fade away from this scene
Everything that is said
just seems to be so mean

I miss my spouse so
but it was her choice to go away
So I deal with the here and now
and my thoughts, not knowing what to say

I Feel Like A Mouse
Continued

I am just a meek person
quiet and humble to the core
I will sit here in my little world
eventually I will open up my door

E. Wayne Searles

I Sit Here Thinking

Random thoughts
selfless good embodied within
My thoughts keep flowing
not knowing where my actions should begin

All of my functions
held back by a moderate feeling
I sit here thinking
as I look at the ceiling

Crushed by feelings
torn between reality and fate
Not knowing what to say
is what I really hate

Consumption is an issue
perceptions out of tune
If I were outside
I'd be starring at the moon

Sometimes I panic
it is what I must not do
I would be much better off
just sharing my thoughts with you

That would be a start
where my actions should begin to flow
All of my selfless good
definitely will begin to show

I Sit Here Thinking
Continued

Taking a deep breath
I start to look around
My perceptions are regained
to a world so profound

E. Wayne Searles

In Disbelief

I don't know where to start
but have so many words to say
So sick and tired
of the hatred in our world today

People have crossed the line
rioting and looting, trying to share some view
The only thing that's on the news
is violence and death and what the government will pursue

The internet is full of whack jobs
posting stories saying the end of time is near
I am so tired of all of this noise
it only causes unwanted hatred and fear

What happened to society
that the world has ended up in such a way
People are just so fed up with lies
it's what we hear every single day

It's hard to have a belief
that we can vote for anyone that will be true
They tell us what we want to hear
then after they are elected they just say phuck you

Our children's futures are at risk
leaving not much hope for freedom and peace for them
The hatred just keeps building
to each other all we do is condemn

In Disbelief
Continued

I'm not sure if this path can be changed
perhaps it's supposed to be this way
I only wish I could close my eyes
and all the hatred, lies, and deceit would all go away today

Jaded Reality

Blessed be my soul
as it resides in this place like Hell
If this is reality
please do tell

Life like a dream world
never knowing what is next
The same illusion you have
when buried in your phone making many text

Technology has become
a control in which we have been fed
To keep us puppets in line
reality seems so dead

Confusion and chaos
nobody wants to believe what could be true
Everyone wants to believe
life is just normal for me and you

Between global warming
and the big hole in the ozone layer
Governments cover up their actions
and send soldiers here and there

Life is no longer normal
on this planet we call earth
Children are having children
and nobody is being responsible for a child's birth

Jaded Reality
Continued

Racism is gaining momentum
everyone being turned against each other
The ashes from this hell
is causing a smell that makes us smother

Where is that reality
that once was not a hell bent dream
Where life was normal
and everything was what it did seem

E. Wayne Searles

Tearful Moments

Enduring emotions
sometimes can be hard to do
Especially when you hear a story
that hits home to you

It could be about family or friends
something recent or from long ago
When it is a heartfelt tragedy
it really hits you so

Sadness is part of life
getting through it, is a task all alone
Even if it's from the loss of a loved one
or memories that chill you to the bone

The very point of this poem
is that being emotional is not so bad
It only shows you're human
and that you can manage to be happy or sad

Emotions can make you stronger
if you manage them in a special way
Don't be afraid to cry
on any given day

Tears cleanse the soul
they rinse away emotions we endure
They allow us to know our hearts
how good and how pure

Just A Child

He just stood there
his head glancing up and says daddy why?
What have I done?
to make you look sad and cry.

I know you love me
and want the best of everything for me
I am only ten
and don't understand everything, you see.

I am just a child
your child and I know you love me dear.
Please take my hand
and wipe away your tear.

I am very sorry
I did not understand it was wrong.
You tell me many times
as if you're singing a song.

Daddy, I am just a child
I don't comprehend everything that you say.
Please slow down
maybe explain it to me in another way.

Daddy,
I really want to be a good boy.
I love you too
not just because you buy me a toy.

Just A Child
Continued

Our relationship is so precious
I am happy to have a dad like you.
There are times when I will be bad
and I will have to pay my due.

Daddy, it's okay that you spanked me
my feelings are hurt, but I know now, I was wrong.
I really will try to understand
so you won't have to sing me that unhappy song.

Son, I know you're growing
and there is so much for you to learn.
We do have a good relationship
and the bridges we shall not burn.

Dear son, you know I love you
thanks for wiping away my tear.
Give me a big hug
very big like hugging a bear.

Son, every day I watch you grow
and one day you will turn into a man.
During this time
for you, I will do everything I can.

So son,
I may set here and cry.
I may have spanked you,
but I always tell you the reason why?

Just A Child
Continued

Let's take a walk
and go have some fun
Wipe away the sadness
now that you understand what you have done.

Thank you daddy
I would love that, it means a lot to me.
While we are at it
I will tell you what I want to be.

Well daddy
It's getting late and it's time for bed
Please smile and be happy
I now understand everything you have said.

E. Wayne Searles

Just A Simple Mistake

Just a simple mistake
and you stab me with spite
Not even thinking
that somehow I might be right

Whether I am right or wrong
I spoke what I believed to be true
I should have been more careful
how I conveyed those words to you

We were once friends
but you cut me loose
With those words you spoke
you hang me from a noose

Still undecided who burnt this bridge
whether it was you or it was me
It really doesn't matter anymore
it's time to just let it be

I cherish my friendship
with each and every friend
Offering a hand of help
and over backwards I will bend

But when a friend damn's me to hell
in a very hateful way
That bridge has been burned
there is nothing more to say

Just A Simple Mistake
Continued

Sentimental I am
it's painful for a friend to lose
I made a simple mistake
but this is what you choose

E. Wayne Searles

Sense Of Confusion

I find myself in a sense of confusion
it happens from day to day
It's as if my brain is being drained
in some iconic way

Aging beholds me
more broken and brittle as time goes by
It seems I train my thoughts
to just keep asking why

Allowance of freedom
within a world created in my head
There is a sense of confusion
of how much time do I have before I am dead

A sense of freedom
would be to just let my thoughts be clear
To stop thinking of death
and how fast time goes by each and every year

Time has its boundaries
we all will have our time to go
Until that time comes
we should all live life and enjoy the show

My Deepest Fear

Tonight I have realized my deepest fear
and now I cannot sleep
I fear death
and it runs so very deep

Having lost loved ones
without being able to say good bye
Not being able to hold their hand
as the angels take them to the sky

So much emotion built up
but hiding it deep within
Tonight I feel something different
and I don't even know where to begin

Some people can handle death
they can even handle blood and gore
I have to turn my cheek to these things
otherwise within me I am damaged a whole lot more

I have seen enough carnage
burned and mangled bodies to some extent
But I keep my images to myself
internal emotions churning, with anger I do vent

I truly love life
finding it so sad, we all have to someday die
I hope somebody holds my hands
when the angels come and take me to the sky

My Deepest Fear
Continued

I know this seems sad
but what I write is so real
I write with words of honesty
I write with words everyone can feel

I am so sorry mother
that I was not there by your side
My heart aches with every thought of you
ever since the day you died

I miss you so much
I was your baby boy to the end
You were my dear mother
and you were my best friend

I find life a hard task
with so much negative emotions deep within
I try so hard to smile
but only manage to grin

Honestly I am scared
not knowing what's on the other side
But the pain I bare in this life
comes from built up emotions that I hide

Often I cannot sleep
as I think of many things from my past
Then I realize how much time I waste
as it slips by so very fast

My Deepest Fear
Continued

Some people are strong
and some people are as cold as ice
I find myself to be very meek
offering a helping hand and being very nice

Now I know for sure
my deepest fear after all
I am afraid to die
so I live behind this wall

I hope I can tear it down
before it's too late
I hope I can find a sense of healing
before I have sealed my fate

May all my demons go away
to leave me with no more fears
So I can enjoy life from here on out
for the remainder of my years

E. Wayne Searles

My Existence

I may have an aged and crippled body
but through my veins blood does still flow
It seems I am a bother to you
and you're ready for me to go

You may not feed me
or realize I have a thirst
The tears of sadness I cry
will make my bladder burst

To drink my tears
fills the hunger from being starved
These memories of all of this
in your mind shall be carved

Fret not my child
I forgive you for your shame
I am your one and only mother
just remember my name

Sadness and sorrow
create this silence I am in
I am sorry to have burdened you
soon a new journey I will begin

I will leave this body
the broken vessel that it may be
I will find peace and happiness elsewhere
where ever my spirit decides to take me

My Existence
Continued

It's your turn
take my sorrow and feel my pain
It is now yours
I hope it doesn't make you go insane

My Silence / Your Fight

How do you do it
to go from being shy to speaking your mind
I will tell you it isn't easy
that is something you will find

It takes a lot of practice
or rather many years
It takes a lot of heart ache
and a whole lot of tears

It takes finding yourself
and knowing who the person is that you are
Then you can get on track
and finally get through things that are so bizarre

The world is a crazy place
once you enter it, leaving your sacred place behind
You will find yourself wishing you hadn't
searched for this new world to find

Trying to grasp the reality
as it's too late to turn back the hands of time
The new life you invoke
is like trying to walk through a path of gooey slime

Your outer emotions may have changed
but inside, you are sorry for the way things turned out
This instance holds rebellion
it makes you want to shout

My Silence / Your Fight
Continued

Being shy isn't so seriously bad
it holds a character of you in special light
It gives you a sense of stability
when others only want to fight

E. Wayne Searles

No Promise Of Tomorrow

It is said tomorrow is never promised
I find these words to be so true
As life can be taken away in an instant
and there is nothing anyone can do

It is heart wrenching
to lose a loved one or a very dear friend
Not having a chance to say good bye
never knowing their time was at en end

Every day we live
is a blessing we may not see
Tomorrow is not promised
it is something now that is very clear to me

Saying I love you
is a very important thing to say
It allows others to know
you love them in every way

Times can be tragic
when someone we love is taken away
It's even more tragic when tomorrow comes
and our final goodbye we cannot say

When you love someone
make sure you let them know
Say the words out loud
let your true feelings show

No Promise Of Tomorrow
Continued

Every day we wake up
to be thankful we should truly be
This message is in a heartfelt way
and something I hope you can truly see

"Tomorrow is today's dream"

E. Wayne Searles

Pierced By A Sword

Today I feel the pain
of a mighty sword piercing my heart
People in this world
starved until this world they depart

Fury within me
burns hotter than any flame
The people responsible
do not have an ounce of shame

How could a human being
say that starving another is the best way
If they continue to feed that person
they could live another day

God is the creator
he giveth and taketh away
When it's a person's time to go
it's not according to what any doctor has to say

This sword hurts me plenty
my heart so burdened with pain
I feel it tearing on the inside
as my blood pours from every vein

Some people have no compassion
remorse they cannot feel
All hell is about to break loose
as they stick me with this sword of steel

Pierced By A Sword
Continued

I have compassion
a humanitarian I am at best
There is remorse for your decisions
of starving a person and laying them to rest

E. Wayne Searles

The Darkness Behind Me

A dark shadow
cast from behind the presence of me
It's nothing more than a dreary past
of nothing more that I want to see

The birds flock around me
to fill a hunger they patiently wait
They come from the shadows
searching for food from my un-devoured fate

The land looks so baron
a desolate place to live
The future looks so bright
what's behind me, to nobody I would give

As I walk
the ground turns to dust
I keep moving ahead of the shadows
or I will fulfill the bird's wildest lust

If the darkness should prevail
and my presence swallowed by the dark
I will leave my scriptures for all to see
it will be my final mark

If the winds of change
should cover what is written for all to see
Then memories of me
were just not meant to be

The Darkness Behind Me
Continued

But the darkness will not prevail
I shall not be swept away
The birds will die of hunger
and I will live another day

E. Wayne Searles

The pain Is Always There

Every day I deal with so much pain
but I still shed a smile
I don't know how much more I can take
I don't know if I can walk another mile

It's been twenty or so years
that my brain just absorbs the pain
I don't believe in medication
it's just a mask and there is nothing to gain

No matter what I do to help it
it's too late, the damage has been done
I just keep on living my life
it's half the battle being won

There are some days
when I am pain free for a while
These are the days I rejoice
when I am so loving, but shedding a true smile

There are three types of pain
they are in my spine, stomach, and head
If I didn't use the mind over matter theory
I would already be dead

When you look at me
you really haven't a clue
How much pain I am in
because I only smile back at you

The Pain Is Always There
Continued

You see, I love life
no matter how much pain there is to bare
I know there are many others with such pain
that's why these words I do share

E. Wayne Searles

WHY?

I think about today
I think about all the time that has gone by
I think about the folks that have left us
I sometimes ask the Lord why

To imagine the reality of time
to fully understand how quickly it goes by
Yesterday we were born
we never know when we will die

It's certainly a sad thing
it fills us with anger and pain to the core
It sometimes makes us hate God
and a whole lot more

When we lose a loved one
were left with a huge void in our heart and mind
We constantly ask ourselves why
but there are no answers to our questions to find

To fathom what we have each day
not always being happy with love and joy inside
We don't realize life is very short
so we better enjoy the ride

There is nothing we can do
to change the plan or the way
There is a path for everyone
I believe in fate I can truly say

WHY?
Continued

They say time heals all wounds
but it's hard when we lose someone we truly love
With all the hurt that follows
we should never lose our faith in God above

E. Wayne Searles

Unexpectedly

I was given sad news today
the news of someone's death
It happened so unexpectedly
they have taken their very last breath

I was in shock
I had no words to say
I am feeling very somber
having no idea I would receive this news today

It makes you realize
you never know when your time is going to be
This is something I have not really thought about
but today it's something I certainly can see

I knew this person for a very short time
but it's still sad to see him go
In my somber mood I bow my head
and pray that, with the Lord he is so

Sometimes we lose people
some are close and others we may barely know
Either way
it is very sad to see any of them go

Tormented From Your Soul

An emotional wreck
feeling the pain from your soul
As it tears at your flesh
because its freedom you stole

Bound and gagged
within your body it is caged
You feel the pain from torn flesh
your soul is outraged

Maybe if you give it freedom
allow your soul to speak
Release your inner energy
and freedom your soul will seek

Imagine being caged
and not being able to say a single word
You would be full of anger too
nothing about it is absurd

Find a sense of peace
with your mind, body, and soul to be as one
Then you will feel the inner torment go away
because freedom your soul will have won

Put at ease the ravaged soul
tranquility is the key
It will no longer tear at your flesh
it will finally let you be

E. Wayne Searles

Why Sad Poetry

Why do you write about suicide
it's something subliminally I can hear you say
You think my thoughts are so deep
as I write about yours on any given day

My name is Wayne
a sensitive person, it is meant for me
Grasping the feelings of others
there are things I can clearly see

Having once been silent
through my own youthful years
I too was bullied
and had my own lake of tears

I managed to get through it
I somehow found strength to deal with the pain
So now I write about dark feelings
to touch the hearts of those that bullies drain

If my words can save a life
and have meaning to a person so very sad
Then I would say writing about suicide is a good thing
I wouldn't say it's boring or bad

People who live a normal life
may not grasp what it is I say
These are the people
who do not live in sadness and fight to live another day

Why Sad Poetry
Continued

So when you find my poetry to be sad
then know the words are not meant for you
It is me as a poet
sending a lifeline, trying to get a message through

Chapter Three

Cherish Family And Friends

Let there not be another day
when we pass by an old friend
Because time has mysterious ways
of bringing life to an abrupt end

Now, more than ever
I feel frightened of that very day
When the time comes
and the good Lord takes me away

Life, as precious as it is
is really shorter than we want it to be
So stop and take the time to say hello
to any friend that you see

Most of us are usually on the run
very busy from day to day
Not realizing how much time has passed
and how quickly any of us can be taken away

Very shocked
I just sit here not knowing what to say
So I will tell you all I love you
I mean it in a very special way

E. Wayne Searles

How Do You See Me

I am a master
reality escapes me not
I know what I have
and what I haven't got

Silence beholds your mouth
words with held within you
You want to speak your peace
if it's the last thing you do

Anger tends to build
as you cannot release thoughts from your mind
Being blatantly direct
is the moment that you will find

Even if it seems I am lost
I am something you will never find
I have a sense of reality
it's truly one of a kind

I am a master
of my own identity
I am a master
of how I want you to see

Blatantly I do not pose
I randomly act the way I think I should be
I tend to be careless
because I don't care, what reality you see

How Do You See Me
Continued

Feel me
grasp what it is that I expose
I wonder how smart you are
my self-being is right under your nose

E. Wayne Searles

Let Me Help You

Hello
hold up your head and look at me
I am here to help
this I want you to see

Alone in this world
feeling so much hate and pain
Having nowhere to go
nothing to cover you from the cold rain

Take my hand
let me help you to stand on your feet
Allow yourself to trust me
and together this cruel world you can beat

Life is precious
when you have the will to live
This is why I want to help you
if only me, your hand you will give

I will take away the clouds
and allow sun to shine on you
Finding love and warmth
is something you will do

This path you have walked
has come to an end today
It's your time to be happy
I will help you in every way

Let Me Help You
Continued

Let me help you
to remove the hate from being so kind
Let me rebuild your trust
that you lost and made you blind

E. Wayne Searles

Look At Yourself

I often ask myself why
wondering who I really am
Always being so judgmental
finding at times I just don't give a damn

Who was I as a child
who am I on this very day
Am I so different than other people
I often wonder, by the words they say

Without any further judgment
upon this person that is me
Look deep within yourself
to see what you can see

You tend to have a bitter heart
and pursue a happiness that is not true
You tend to break down others
and steal their energy just for you

So as I sit here and wonder
I do not need to question anything of me
I just need to find happiness
and ignore you negative rationality

Every single person
is beautiful in their very own way
The only thing that makes them so ugly
is with negative words that they say

Look At Yourself
Continued

The only difference I can see
between my childhood and now
I have had an incredible journey
the only true word is "WOW"

E. Wayne Searles

Medication Is A Mask

Being alive
is the greatest gift we get
Knowing how to live this life is important
without having any regret

A life without any pain
would not be the greatest life of all
Not having any hurt
every time we take a fall

We would lose our sense of reality
leaving us feeling immortal and cold
Never knowing when we hurt others
making all of us feeling way too bold

I like pain
mastering it, is controlling how you feel
Medicating yourself to oblivion
takes your pain away, but your health it will steal

Medication is just a mask
a mask I refuse to wear
My mind is of strong will
of my body and pain it will take care

Grasping the sensation of pain
allows you to grasp being alive as well
There will be times when it hurts so bad
putting on the mask of medication is where you will dwell

I Apologize My Friend

You ruined my day
or so I thought it was so
However that's not totally true
it's about the way I wanted to go

I don't always listen
to what other people have to say
So it seems
it was I that ruined my day

Easy to point a finger
to blame someone else for anything wrong
Easy to say it's your fault
all of the day long

Being angry
not having a clear thought in my head
You were in the wrong place at wrong time
it's your fault, are the words in my head constantly being said

Eventually my mind will clear
my faults will inevitably ascend
Then I will feel my guilt
for being a jerk to a very good friend

I hate it when this happens
sometimes I lose control of things I do
I hope you will forgive me
as I apologize to you

E. Wayne Searles

Missing You My Friend

I can't break it
I can't break this dwelling
I have a pain in my heart
and it just keeps swelling

My mind just keeps thinking
I don't know how to stop it from doing so
Many memories flashing through my mind
of a dear friend, it was his time to go

I am very sad
when I am suppose to rejoice
Even though he is gone
I still hear my dear friend's voice

He had such a love for life
and had so much positive energy to share
His first words were always "Hey Man"
from a man that was always very sincere

This is so very hard
but as everyone, I take it day by day
If I had one wish to be granted
it would have been one last goodbye, before he went away

It is said that time heals
and memories will make us all smile
I only wish it were possible
to have coffee with my friend and chat for a while

Missing You My Friend
Continued

I know that is not possible
so I will have to cherish those memories in my mind
I will never forget my brother Mark
he was a great friend, absolutely one of a kind

Rest In Peace
Mark Thomas Shelly

E. Wayne Searles

No Shame In Crying

My eyes swell with tears
something I read, touched my heart today
It opened up that hidden pain
that I thought had gone away

Suppressed deep inside
from a loss not so long ago
I have been living in pain
and I didn't even know

Wandering around in daily life
just another lost sheep in the herd
My thinking has been foggy
to me, none of this has even occurred

We may think crying is shameful
but it's healthier than you know
It opens up your heart and mind
every time you let those tears flow

There is no shame in crying
there is a beauty of it all
It's a reaction to help you
just before you fall

Keep your memories
that are so dear to each of you
Just release the pain inside
allowing tears to flow, will get you through

Flavor Of Life

Every day we taste life
it is ever so bitter sweet
The flavor changes
with everyone we meet

Blind ambitions
like an apple not far from a tree
Some people will try to fool
not realizing what we can see

Carrying a smile
I keep life at it's simple best
If I can manage it
maybe others too, should give drama a rest

The flavor of the day
Pineapple sure would do
Change your ambitions
and allow true sweetness through

Life is short
so try and carry a smile
Don't let your flavor be sour
by being in denial

Every day can be sweet
it's all about the ingredients you add
So smile and be happy
and your ambitions won't be bad

Saying I Love You

I love you
words so easy to say
Not always meant by some
their feelings they can't relay

Three words together
very strong indeed
Spoken with true feeling
receiving them back we all need

I say I love you
but you do not respond
These words I speak to you
are words of which you are not very fond

My actions express how I feel
my emotions burn
I know that I love you
it's these words from you I yearn

I don't want to beg you
I should be able to see how you feel
I should not push you
your false feelings I do not want to steal

Why do you keep me
and feed me false hope on which to inspire
It's a shame your heart's cold as ice
while my hearts on fire

Saying I Love You
Continued

Maybe it's about time
for me to be strong with less emotion
Maybe it's time to stop saying I love you
when there is no pledge of devotion

E. Wayne Searles

Time To Break Your Fall

The world around you looks so familiar
family life is looking very strange
The love you once had
its focus is way out of range

Wanting time to be alone
to manage built up frustration that's within
Finding yourself doing crazy stuff
and always having no idea where to begin

Not knowing, is the worst
being indecisive because you feel somewhat lost
Making decisions because of built up anger
the outcome could have a high cost

You seem to be falling
and you don't even know
The crazy world is more familiar
as you feel like you have nowhere else to go

Your family still loves you
something of which you are totally aware
It's the communication that's a problem
and it causes you to not care

The world can offer just so much
and your family can offer you so much more
It's time to change your thoughts
and return to those you truly adore

Time To Break Your Fall
Continued

Life is crazy
every day new stories are made
Find peace and love with your family
making memories that will never fade

It's time to break your fall
otherwise you're going to crash and burn
Find peace within your mind
it is of great concern

E. Wayne Searles

Times Can Be Hard

Why do we try so hard
only to be broken down again
Trying to be loving
staying away from a world of sin

Times can be hard
and times can be great
Life can be hard
when we don't know our fate

We live in our own pasture
our own world to which we graze
Trying to control our inner feelings
from being broken on certain days

If we allow ourselves to falter
to be broken and feel so bad
We can only blame ourselves
for the reasons that make us sad

We try so hard
because we want to be happy and succeed
We want to have positive energy
and not have a heart that may always bleed

No matter who you are
trying hard is something you should always do
Even if you have solemn days
when you feel broken, and don't feel like being you

Times Can Be Hard
Continued

Never give up
graze your pasture with great pride
Others will like what they see
and will be happy to be by your side

Unknown To Yourself

Bitter
bitter is the cold
Bitter is the words
that your mouth unfold

Elaborate
elaborate is the way you speak
It is the way you poise yourself
and you look so unique

Confusion
confusion is disorder when I think
It's how you make me feel
I stare without a blink

Disbelief
disbelief is my illusion
The words you speak
are my negative infusion

I can't bare
to withstand the likes of you
Your presence
it makes my blood boil and stew

You're just cold
how is it you are this way
Take the hand of a loving friend
let go of your bitterness today

Unknown To Yourself
Continued

Remain elaborate
in every single way
Just be more careful
with the sharp spoken words that you say

Words To A Selfless Friend

The flowers are so beautiful
thank you for thinking of me
It's something you didn't have to do
but it's what you wanted to be

You often think of others
not putting yourself first
If you had the last glass of water
you'd give it to another, if they had a deeper thirst

Your selflessness is amazing
you are unique in every way
A truly loving person
you have a special gift I'd say

So thank you for the flowers
and having me on your mind
You are so filled with love
you are one of a kind

Your friendship is truly honored
you're such a blessing in disguise
Whenever I am down
you help my spirits again rise

May God give you blessings
in everything that you do
You deserve a gift as well
so I send all my love to you

Words To A Selfless Friend
Continued

I don't have any flowers
but have many words to say
So to you my friend
I share these words to you today

E. Wayne Searles

What Is Reality

To grasp reality
or to think there is such a thing
Is like breaking silence
when you know it's going to sting

Is reality of normalcy
or is it just a world of its own
Is it a place where people think everything is right
to where nobody should cast a single stone

How wretched are the ones
thinking their reality is so normal
That others need to follow suit
and be equally so formal

Let the truth to be told
reality is nothing but a world in which we all create
It's about how are lives all revolve
in this world of love and hate

Beyond any realm of our minds
is to be beyond any such thing as reality
There is a state of eccentric
an unknown form of normality

Everyone has a normal life
based on how they believe they should live it through
It's a personal sense of reality
I really believe it to be true

What Is Reality
Continued

So I grasp my sense of reality
even though it may be different than how you believe
There truly is no normal way to live
where equally, it's a world we all can conceive

E. Wayne Searles

Feeling Of A Nice Day

The sun starting to rise
the earth turns around it with the light breaking the plain
There are not many clouds in the sky
it's looking like no chance of rain

The air feeling cool
fresh with the morning breeze
Amazing how the seasons change
the spring's pollen makes me sneeze

A cup of coffee
soon setting on my table
Maybe a slice of toast or two
if I can only stop sneezing and I'm able

Breakfast is down
coffee tasted really great
Time to clean the house
I need to finish it before eight

The kid's lunches are packed
now they are outside waiting for the bus
This is my time for cleaning
now that is a plus

It's after eight
the cleaning has been done
Now it is my time
to go out and relax and catch some sun

Feeling Of A Nice Day
Continued

Oh I love warm weather
especially on days like today
I only wish it could stay like this
and never go away

The day has passed
the sun a blessing to us all
Before we know it
it will be summer then comes fall

I have enjoyed this day
taking in the sun by each and every ray
Evening has come
time for this day to go away

Watching out the window
as the sun sets in the western sky
At times it's a breathtaking view
that I cannot deny

Darkness is about to cover us
as the sunlight falls out of sight
It is now time to end this poem
and time to say good night

E. Wayne Searles

Deep Blue Sky

As I stand alone
staring into the deep blue sky
I see clouds that look like figures
as they slowly drift on by

At times like this
a world of wonder is where I seem to be
Falling into a daydream state
allowing me my thoughts to see

Reality of life
or facts about the things we do
Losing a grip
is only done by me or you

Insight and knowledge
gained from many things we do
At times we need a break
so we stare off into the big old blue

Standing alone is ok
but it's better to have a friend by your side
Share with them your hopes and dreams
as if you have nothing to hide

So take a look at the beautiful sky
and your thoughts will start to flow
If you find your answers there
only you or your friend will know

Deep Blue Sky
Continued

Find tranquility and peace
to relax your busy mind
Things will somehow seem clearer
this you will certainly find

FATE

Sitting here, I wonder
about the path I have chosen
Thoughts seem a bit blurry
and are a bit frozen

It seems like destiny
has a fate for me unknown
For this path I have chosen
is leaving me feeling so alone

Even though this is my feeling
I have children to love me so
They only know that I'm their daddy
and they need my returning love to make them glow

There is such a negative charge
pushing down on my soul
It seems to be this place I'm in
feeling like I cannot go

I am at a point
where the pressure is too great
I feel the need to travel
to seek my true fate

A Sagittarius I am
born under the sign of the sun
I only want to travel
away from my family I will not run

FATE
Continued

When life gets to a point
where a person has to wonder who they are
It is truly a time to evaluate
the path they have traveled thus far

I know I have an absence
my mind tells me so
On the 14th of July
it will be time to go

I will return
when my freedom allows me to
I love you all
and promise to come back to you

E. Wayne Searles

My Path

You see this road I walk
it's narrow and covered with stones
After I walk this road for so long
it puts an aching to my weary bones

However, to stop walking
I will not do
It's a path to my destiny
where self pride is bright and true

Bruised and sore
my feet bleed a bit too
I just keep walking this road
it's all I know to do

To myself I give allegiance
staying strong with a sense of pride
This long road I walk is beautiful
no thank you, I do not need a ride

There is so much to see
and there is so much to learn
There are many surprises
around each and every turn

No road is forever straight
many turns and hills to walk
Occasionally along the way
you will meet people who love to talk

My Path
Continued

This old dirt road
which offers pain I can endure
You lead me to my future
it's a path that is not obscure

A narrow road you are
however a beautiful site for me
As I sometimes look back
many beautiful memories I can see

Music Makes Me Feel

The music
it soothes my soul today
Remembering my childhood
it seems so far away

Trying to understand life
but it certainly confuses me
So I just listen to oldies music
it takes me where I want to be

Good Night
no, I can't sleep
I just listen to the music
it sometimes makes me weep

Sometimes I am not so strong
sensitivity creeps my way
Needing to clear my mind
I search for things to say

My body may be getting old
but my mind lives in a time years ago
I miss those days so much
I have to say it's so

Forgive me for my moment
sadness took control
The music took me away
it helps to soothe my soul

Music Makes Me Feel
Continued

There is nothing wrong with sadness
it allows you to feel
Emotions are good to have
knowing how to use them can help you heal

E. Wayne Searles

Life Can Be Rough As A Teen

A portion of my life was stolen
many years ago
It suddenly became clear tonight
after watching a TV show

I have been living my life blind
no regrets to have lived this way
I didn't know my true feelings
I just lived day by day

I had so much love
but never received the same
I was always made to look like an idiot
and always put in the way of shame

Eventually I started acting out
the ways I was made to feel
Always belittled by others
however, my fate they did not seal

As a teen, I once ran away
but I did not make it very far
Wanting to change my life
that was overwhelmingly bizarre

I managed to climb many mountains
being harassed was only an inspiration to me
It only made me stronger
giving me courage I once did not see

Life Can Be Rough As A Teen
Continued

Life is full of surprises
and being a teen can really be rough
There are many times
when you will feel you've had enough

Take a deep breath
think twice and call a friend
Tell them you need to talk
it doesn't have to be the end

E. Wayne Searles

No Rays Of Sunlight

What if all it does is rain
no sunshine to dissipate that dark cloud
No rays of sunlight
just crackling thunder that's so loud

How could we possibly be happy
or find a smile from such a day
When all we wish for is sunshine
praying the rain will just go away

I think our lives would be sad
however the sun does shine through
The clouds do go away
so we don't always feel so blue

Nature is amazing
life is a very special thing
How we all live it
is our very own song to sing

So if you choose to be sad
on a bright sunny day
It will be raining in your world
even when the clouds go away

What if it rains
more than the sun does shine
Then we need to shake of that saddening feeling
that puts shivers down our spine

No Rays Of Sunlight
Continued

Try to find some happiness
a smile will stop your flow of tears
This lovely life we have been given
is only for a certain amount of years

E. Wayne Searles

Steps To Tranquility

Another step
of every step I take
I walk into another realm of reality
where nothing is fake

Everything around me is real
at natures very best
Beyond this place I invade
its existence I would have never guessed

So peaceful
I quietly step further from my entry point
The sounds of nature invade me
my body it does anoint

My eyes get weary
I relax and fall to the ground
In total concentration
I fall asleep in this place I am bound

Time has passed
I have awaken, thinking it was all a dream
I open my eyes gently
to see streaks of the sunlight gleam

Just another walk in the forest
where I often love to go
This is where my footsteps lead me
it's such a peaceful place to know

Steps To Tranquility
Continued

To have such a place
where you can put total ease to your mind
It will give you tranquility
and a sense of relaxation that is so hard to find

E. Wayne Searles

Tomorrow Never Promised

Tomorrow is never promised
why is it, this we never see
Today, to us was given
Tomorrow, may never be

The future is vague
only made with a plan you see
Tomorrow is never promised
to you or to me

So I make a new pledge
to remove any hate from within
To work toward a tomorrow
a new plan to begin

I know it's not promised
but I will do my best to make it so
Life on this earth is short
at any time we can go

At times we get angry
and from our mouths spew words of hate
We need to open our eyes and see
tomorrow is nothing more than fate

Love and respect each other
having no remorse from yesterday
So if tomorrow does come
sorry is a word you won't have to say

Daddy why are you so angry

Daddy why are you so angry
I hate to see you this way
What can I do to help
is there something I can say

Son I am sorry I seem so angry
I do not mean to be this way
I do not mean to scare you
by anything I do or say

I'm not sure how to explain it
but daddy is hurt inside
Just know that I still love you
and my arms are opened wide

Daddy I know that you love me
I know that you're hurting too
I try to understand it
really daddy I do

I am just a child
so I may not fully understand
I will try not to fear your anger
now daddy, please hold my hand

Son I truly love you
you are the sunshine I truly need
You are the band aid
whenever I am hurt and I bleed

"Dedicated to all Veterans dealing with PTSD"

Chapter Four

My Silence

Silence
Doesn't mean you, I ignore
It means I am in a special place
only I can adore

Sometimes it's a place
where I have to be
It's a place
where no others can see

The sound of silence
brings peace to mind
It helps to empty
negativity of any kind

Silence
a meditation for mind
You should find your place there too
it will help you unwind

Thank you for understanding
why I seem so distant at times like I do
It's just about me
and is nothing against you

I will be okay
just a need to be let be
It's my way of daily healing
it's what sets me free

E. Wayne Searles

A Place To Heal

Oh what a beautiful tree
the landscape is so breath taking as well
I could make paintings
to capture this and sell

The nature is so wild
full of life beyond what we know
For walks in the nature
is where I often love to go

So much inner healing
comes from being put at ease
I am so fortunate
I can see the animals, birds, flowers, and the trees

I hear the chirping sounds
as birds make their playful calls
Once I have entered a forest
I do not want to leave from its inner walls

Oh what a sanctuary
where peace of mind can be found
It's too sad
that to a stressful world most are bound

So I stand here and wonder
before I walk into the nature today
I wonder of the beauty
of how it takes my stressful feelings away

A Place To Heal
Continued

Finding a contented heart
each and every time I go
It helps me heal on the inside
this, I want you all to know

E. Wayne Searles

A Related Pain

Again, Slightly on the rise
energy from a soul that burns
Tired of this world in which it lives
fighting hatred and pain everyone so yearns

Every day is agonizing
but somehow I make it through the day
I try to ignore the media
and the fake games in which they play

What happened to a world
in which I used to live, not so many years ago
The newer generation has killed it
a lack of parental obedience will tell you so

Some days it's hard to raise my head
to see what's going on around
Tired of living in a sense of fear
that terror is coming to yet another town

Anxiety has grown deep within
not allowing me to sleep at night
My burning soul has too much energy
and my body doesn't know how to use it right

Lashing out at people
because of negativity inside of me
Having such a built up hatred
allowing no creativity

A Related Pain
Continued

A suppressed entity
will leave me the day I die
It will haunt the likes of others
and they will often wonder why

If only I knew how to change it
to douse the flame of a burning soul within
I could change my emotional visions
somehow managing to live in this world of sin

E. Wayne Searles

Curiosity Of The Deep

The depth of me
uncertain to anything outside the walls of my mind
The illusions built within my territory
a world you will never find

Calculated rhythms
daily running through my head
They never ever stop
not even when I go to bed

As long as my heart keeps pumping
it will constantly feed my brain
This universe in which I live
I assure is not so mundane

I shine bright from within
but that light never leaves the edges of my soul
It leaves me locked up in my world
living like a troll

My sanity is your curiosity
leaving you speechless in every way
You just can't see who I truly am
so a distance away you will stay

Seemingly a dark soul
however innocence lies deep inside
I cater to your humor
only in myself I do confide

Curiosity Of The Deep
Continued

Don't rattle your thoughts
about the certain likes of me
If you manage to break these chains
who knows what you may set free

E. Wayne Searles

Here In This Place I Lay

Every face is blank
but on the shadow, every facial expression I can see
This is the world in which I travel
and the visions for which I see

I lay here in this place
dark and dreary like a dungeon, I would have to say
It is very silent here
except for the noises piercing the silence today

Immobilized
with pain from head to toe
I cannot get out of this bed
if I did, I would have nowhere to go

My world is slowly changing
I'm just not the person I used to be
That's why faces seem so blank
and on the shadows, the faces I can see

It's all about imminent change
everything of which we cannot control
It's like finishing the chapter in a book
and then onto the next page we scroll

These moments, seemingly delusional
probably medication making me the way I feel
Here I lay in confusion
nothing at all seems so real

Here In This Place I Lay
Continued

I wish this was just a dream
and once again I would wake up without any pain
Because this place where I am
will cause me to go insane

E. Wayne Searles

No Means No

How many times
does a person have to say no
Before you push them in a corner
and they have nowhere to go

So brilliant with your ideas
your tongue causes them pain
Because they keep saying no
you're making them insane

Just stop and listen
allow yourself to hear what they say
There must be reasons for saying no
but you just don't obey

Stop lashing out
it's not just your world
Your trying to get ahead
your ideas to be unfurled

No means no
so just back the hell away
If a person will say yes
then just wait for them to say

In the meantime
no is the answer and it's your cue
Try to be more civilized
it's time you finally get a clue

No Means No
Continued

To be harsh is not my way
but defeating you piercing tongue I need to do
I walk from this corner
saying a final no to you

E. Wayne Searles

Not Knowing How To Feel

Sometimes not knowing how to feel
can be the worst feeling
Not knowing which way to turn
because retribution may be in the dealing

Who should I turn to
with these feelings that dwell inside
Are my feelings true
or are they cause from medication of which I tried

How do I know who to trust
as everyone has an agenda of their own
It's why I keep to myself
and my true feelings never shown

Everyone reaches a stage of confusion
that causes them to be blind
Not knowing which way to turn
or not knowing how to unwind

Not knowing how to feel
is just a mechanism built in
It protects us from uncertainty
when our patience is wearing thin

Mixed emotions and anxiety
ingredients to a doomed path for sure
Open yourself up and talk
to keep your mind clean and pure

Not Knowing How To Feel
Continued

Allow your feelings to change
with no focus on anything bad
Just know who you are
and focus on happiness, not being sad

E. Wayne Searles

Not Your Maiden Voyage

My vision
your flight
You don't acknowledge what I say
even though I am right

I am not transparent
I know that's true
Please just listen
when I explain my visions to you

My mind knows
what your eyes need to see
You don't like to listen
so I give you hints subliminally

Having been once in your shoes
I know where it is that you seem to be
You're flying high in your world
these are the visions from me

Taking no advice
out of fear of feeling weak
You know you need help
but help you will not seek

You are the pilot of your destiny
it is you that chooses where you will go
My vision tells me you will get it
and when you do, you will know

Not Your Maiden Voyage
Continued

For you this isn't any maiden voyage
So you may not listen to me
But eventually my friend
my visions you will one day see

E. Wayne Searles

Numbers-Memories-And-Age

One, two, three, four,
growing up and out the door.
Five , six, seven, eight,
taught negative things, and learn to hate.

Nine, ten,
remember back to then.
when learning was important for me,
only when were older, this we see.

The counting has stopped,
life goes on as so.
We grow older,
but not our soul.

Having traveled so far
looking back from time to time.
Much distance from this elder
and what was a childhood of mine.

Having learned to relax
taking life day by day
Having learned that stress
will surely make you pay.

From childhood
to an adult or until I die.
I have learned so many things
and know my memory is a spy.

My memory flashes me pictures
of a very distant past
My memory flashes me pictures
of events that are so vast.

Numbers-Memories-And-Age
Continued

Not being able to forget
many instances of things I have done.
Still being alive
is one gift I have won.

Forty eight years
feeling good for the most part
I am not sure
when again counting I will start.

E. Wayne Searles

Our Wings Fly With Time

Spreading my wings to the essence of time
I believe I can fly
Every time I look back
I ask myself why

In the moments we get caught up
the realm of age we cannot see
Then as time passes by
the wrinkles of our skin show clearly

The winds of time carry us
it carries us so far away
Leaving many memories
so we don't forget each and every day

However there is no guarantee
our memories will not fade away
Once they are gone, they're gone
these wings will not bring us to the past for a day

I certainly don't like the wings of time
I don't like to fly so far on any day
My wrinkles are becoming too many
my memories are starting to fade away

When the wings of time are tired
and we can fly no more
It's off to Heavens gates
with our wings of time we will finally soar

Our Wings Fly With Time
Continued

At that time of our journey
the pain and suffering of this world will go away
We will wait for our loved ones
their wings will too get tired some day

E. Wayne Searles

Penetrating Emotion

I truly share my feelings
expressing how I really feel
Even if they are only through my eyes
a sight of you I did steal

Capturing a glimpse of you
while you're feeling down
I tear open your feelings
entering you without a sound

Trying to figure you out
so I know just what to say
Allowing myself to use special words
that just might brighten up your day

It takes a lot of energy
to grasp what does not belong to me
The reason why I do it
is to help set you free

I have an emotional GPS
it guides me where I need to go
It helps me see how others feel
and help them to feel what they need to know

Sometimes we are blind
to this life that we live
We hide our feelings deep
and turn around when someone offers a hand to give

Penetrating Emotion
Continued

I thank God every day
for this gift he gave to me
So I can speak to all of you
with words that can help you see

E. Wayne Searles

Remaining Calm

I may
I might
But I won't
it just doesn't seem very right

I will hold within
metaphors that will eventually decay
Leaving my mind blank
not having anything else to say

Swarmed with dizziness
feeling somewhat neutral but yet engaged
Trying to maintain good feelings
so I don't become outraged

Wishing for silence
but not as silent as dead of night
I want things to be normal
with all sound and sight

Your saturation of words
show such a display
But I shall refrain from being explicit
being silent for yet another day

It is with much delight
I am able to control what I do
It is with much sadness
to watch others control the likes of you

Remaining Calm
Continued

Creator of my destiny
with the things I do each day
If you gain control of your life
you will too see things in a much better way

E. Wayne Searles

Silence Heals The Soul

The sound of silence
so peaceful it clears my mind
When I'm there it's awesome
until invaded by noise of any kind

Silence brings me to a special place
where visions are better than reality
The sound of silence brings me joy
I get overwhelmed within its serenity

This modern world
in which we live every day
There is not much silence
therefore I often pray

I pray to God to give me peace
and to make changes for all humanity
I pray for moments of silence
so I can close my eyes and see

Our world has become so dark
but no silence can be heard at all
With our eyes open
we only see visions that bring sadness from our fall

We all need to find peace
it starts within us its true
Just closing our eyes in moments of silence
is something we all must do

Silence Heals The Soul
Continued

We don't need our eyes wide open to see
however silence will allow us to truly hear
Humanity needs to change its ways
with these words I couldn't be more sincere

E. Wayne Searles

Skin Deep

I really think I'm smoking
I really think I'm hot
Some think I'm delusional
my self confidence says I'm not

To some I may be ugly
to others I have lots of sex appeal
I am not trying to be someone else
with another identity to steal

I am who I am
the person I was created to be
I am the person in the mirror
and I love what I see

It really doesn't matter
what others think of me
I love myself first
so others can like what they see

Attitude comes from within
and it shines who you are
So portray happy thoughts
it will take you very far

Projection is the key
so it's okay to think you're hot
Even if there are others
that think that you're not

Putting Out the Fire

It's such a wonderful day
happiness in the air
Molten lava below the surface
but those feelings I will not share

Trying to have peace in mind
throughout this lovely day
I can't think of a metaphor
for the things I want to say

I only know this
that my smile will make you happy too
So today I will burn inside
while sharing kindness with each of you

Nobody is perfect
some days can be bad
I just want today to be a happy one
and not to be sad

So let me lift you
and in return, your spirits will also lift me
I may be boiling inside
but we just can't let that be

So I choose enlightenment
as I want to feel happy and free
It will put out that fire
that burns deep inside of me

E. Wayne Searles

Strange Pain

This pain I am feeling
like I have never had before
Not sure when it started
but it hurts more and more

I feel it when I am driving
listening to music that soothes my ear
Finding myself in other places
just not being here

My thoughts are wandering
as I think about my life
Always thinking of my children
always, thinking about my wife.

It is very hard
always being away from who I love
All week long
i find myself praying to God above.

We don't know what we have
if always taken for granted
Sometimes it's hard to tell
if that love, is so deeply planted.

Back to this pain
that resides inside of me
I am not sure where I am
i just know I want it to flee.

At a moment in my life
when things just seem so strange
Losing sight of what I want
it has gone way out of range.

Strange Pain

Continued

I feel as if I sleep
dreaming my life away
Wondering why I traveled so far
and yet here I stay

It seems so pointless
no reason to feel this type of pain
But yet I have this feeling
I hope it is not in vain.

Why do people feel like this
I really want to know
I want to find happiness
and make this feeling go

I know you have read my poem
please don't worry about me
I am very strong
I will shake this pain, you will see.

E. Wayne Searles

Tear Down Your Wall

Back to the countryside
I left so long ago
The doors left open for me
this, I can say is so

Just a travel adventure
going back to where I once did live
Visualizing a difference
I have so many thanks to give

I remember sleeping in my car
In the dead cold
Memories I still have
even though I am growing old

Sitting here thinking
of what is just a memory
Realizing how much different things are
than what they use to be

The emotional stress
from living behind a wall
I just sit here and listen
hearing the voice of it all

A masquerade with confusion
I did not have a plan
Before tearing down that wall
I was in solitude, horrible for any woman or man

Tear Down Your Wall
Continued

Time is what has healed
the wounds around my heart
I was given a new beginning
a chance for a very fresh start

Healing comes from within
allowing yourself to tear down your wall
It is something you absolutely can do
as no wall is ever too tall

E. Wayne Searles

That Critical Moment

That moment
when we realize things are so very wrong
We seem to be slipping through time
just living and listening to the song

The path we walk is tiresome
the pain we endure, we hide
We want to set ourselves free
but don't want that roller coaster ride

Reality is sometimes so harsh
it just laughs in your face
You have no idea why you hang on so long
you just know you have been blind in this place

So many things that you love
but a sense of loneliness swallows your heart
You hate to be alone
and this situation just tears you apart

Your heart says one thing
but your mouth utters a happy song
You fight within yourself every day
this is what's so very wrong

Being afraid
is somewhat the same as being weak
You want to free yourself
because your future at present looks so very bleak

That Critical Moment
Continued

Only you
the master of your very own destiny
It is only you
who can right your wrongs and set yourself free

E. Wayne Searles

The Dreams Of You

You ask yourself
with a very silent voice inside
Why you feel this way
on this journey's ride

Taken to many places
while yet you stay in one
You see it all
the stars, the moon, the darkness, and the shining sun

Somewhat like a dream
only dreams are more your reality
They allow you to live
your dreams are what set you free

Recourse of your actions
often redirect your every move you make
Somehow there is an illusion
between what is real and what is fake

Wondering with deep thought
why you feel this way
Your journey takes you nowhere
repeating what you do every day

Grasping for a conclusion
to find closure in what you feel
The answers are right there
to show you what is real

The Dreams Of You
Continued

Don't be burdened by your journey
it has its place in all that you do
Spend more time living
not analyzing all the dreams of you

E. Wayne Searles

Tick Tock

Tick Tock Tick tock
the second hand turns so slow
Father time doesn't stand still
he's always on the go

An alarm goes off
as you try to stop time
The second hand still keeps on ticking
but you'll still hear the chime

The ticking has a rhythmic nature
it tends to take your mind away
Father time has total control
there's nothing we can do or say

Take a deep breath
Relax and do not stress
It's the beginning of your understanding
that you now have to address

Tick Tock Tick Tock
let the clock tick away
After all my friends
it's just another day

Subterfuge

I've created my own subterfuge
spewing hatred that burns inside
I only hurt everyone around me
I have no fear and do not hide

I travel a lot
but within a world that's my very own place
Black and white seem to be the only colors
that taunt the human race

I have been educated
hatred is my skill
I have no remorse at all
it doesn't bother me to kill

Lives don't matter
my views are weak, but I don't care
My education of hatred helps me
get in my face if you dare

Anarchy is my claim
to be righteous in my own way
If you can prove me wrong
I will allow such subterfuge to go away

E. Wayne Searles

What Is Success

What is success
at what level do we start to have greed
When do we lose sight of what money does
it's such an evil seed

Is success about being rich
or is it about being happy and content with what you do
Is it about getting that special job
the one that's comfortable for you

At what level of success are we happy
where we enjoy life so well
Where we can afford to be comfortable
not worrying about bills and what's next to sell

I see success as a happy place
not that job dreamed of for a long time
It is when you smile each day
but not yet struggling over a dime

It's having a heart full of love
having been brought up knowing right from wrong
Knowing your place in society
being friendly and with everyone, getting along

Success is that motive
that churns inside
When you do all you can
without begging for society to provide

What Is Success
Continued

Success comes from within
it's what you teach your children too
To give them good motivation
the same like you

Having lots of money
doesn't mean, a successful person you are, or will be
It's amazing how many people believe
that having so much money sets you free

E. Wayne Searles

Turn It Around

If I may
if I might
Touch your soul
with words tonight

Your broken soul
I will try to heal
By giving you words to read
that your soul will feel

At times we all feel broken
and have moments of not knowing what to do
Our world crashes upon us
leaving us totally without any clue

Depression creeps upon us
telling us it's not worth it to live
It tears us away from society
we reject help people want to give

We become negative
feeling numb within our shell
Feeling close to calling it quits
and our soul we want to sell

If you are feeling numb
and like there is nothing to live for
It only means change is coming
and for you, there's a whole lot more

Turn It Around
Continued

Fighting the good fight
holding on tight will get you through
Don't let anything bring you down
you're one of a kind, you are you

Things will get better
things will change for the good
The depression and loneliness will go away
then you will live your life as you should

Chapter Five

From The Heavens I Hold Your Hand

The heavens will hold my spirit
the rains will release my tears
All sadness will be gone
also taken, will be my fears

It is sad we have to part ways
eventually our time on earth is done
We pass on our family legacy
to a wonderful daughter or a son

I will be watching over you
listening when you call my name
I may not show up in the flesh
but you will know that I came

I will walk by your side
wipe away your tears when you cry
My body maybe gone
but my spirit didn't die

Just know that I love you
I am so proud of how you all turned out to be
I am in the heavens now
and when you look up, the brightest star will be me

Carry on our memories and traditions
with your chin held high
I know you can do it
you're my loving children, that's the reason why

E. Wayne Searles

Count Your Blessings

Today I am happy
a few days ago I was not
I have come to a realization
to everything I have got

Having been blessed
but sometimes it's just hard to tell
Those are the days we're not happy
when our worlds are broken for a spell

Life feels so lonely
when we have such a day
Then we feel so much anger
and treat everyone in a very bad way

Sometimes we just need to stop
and take a good look around
We need to count our blessings we have
in this world in which we are bound

Our world could be crashing around us
but we should not despair
There's always a light at the end of the tunnel
family and friends are waiting for us there

So today I am very happy
many blessings I do have in this life
The good Lord blessed me
with three wonderful children and a beautiful wife

Count Your Blessings
Continued

So count your blessings
and find happiness inside each of you
Your world will be a much better place
and for everyone else too

E. Wayne Searles

Demons Or Angels

Demons or angels
I don't know what I am suppose to say
Whatever they are
they just won't go away

Buzzing around
deep within my mind
I feel their presence
some are fierce and some are kind

Oh what have I done
why do they always bother me
Just go away
please set me free

This life I live
what is the meaning, I sometimes wonder
I see sunshine with the angels
with the demons I hear thunder

On the inside I fight
while outside I look calm as hell
I will not give in
my soul I will not sell

I will continue this fight
this fierce battle deep within side of me
Eventually I will win
I will set myself free

Demons Or Angels
Continued

Angels are the answer
it's what I am suppose to say
Sunshine is what I want
time for the thunder to go away

E. Wayne Searles

Divine Beauty

Today I looked at myself
I caught a glimpse of my reflection
I did not see ugly or beauty
I only saw perfection

Being blind to how you look
is the key to a happy heart
It's a way to keep emotions in check
so your thoughts don't tear you apart

When we become unhappy
over a simple little flaw or two
We over react with panic
it's what we always do

Beauty is only skin deep
so don't get hung up on your reflection
What you will see
does not need a thorough inspection

Be happy for who you are
you come from a mold that has been broken
Listen to what I say
to you, my wisdom has been spoken

Enjoy your life each day
smile and your beauty will surely shine
Next time you see your reflection
you will see yourself as divine

Divine Beauty
Continued

Just listen to your soul
it will not steer you wrong
You will be very happy
knowing you're where you belong

Do You Believe

The Lord shouts from the heavens
then his teardrops fall from the sky
Saddened by humanities lack of interest
and the fact his presence they do deny

Heartbroken Jesus
his son that died for our sins
To many it's just an elusive story
something that makes those doers of evil to have grins

Then there are the angels
that watch over those in need
I can tell you I'm a believer
having to live in this world of greed

I have never seen God our Lord
never have seen Jesus his one and only son
I just know that the time is coming
and a special place in the heavens for all the hearts they have won

To all of you folks out there
not knowing if there is a heaven or hell
Just believe in the positive
and the lovely stories of God there is to tell

If you're not sure with your faith
and would love to go to a wonderful place when you die
Give your heart to God
and watch his teardrops dry

Do You Believe
Continued

Eternity is forever
a very long time to live in torment and pain
Just find peace within your heart
and give God a place to rein

E. Wayne Searles

Father Of Forgiveness

I have many blessings
blessings from the sky
They come from you oh father
this I cannot deny

Dear father I know you would bless others too
but they just don't believe
The thought of you in nonsense
it's something they just can't conceive

Too many times father
you have spoken to me
You have kept me from harm's way
when it was something I could not see

I am truly sorry
others cannot imagine you are for real
That you are God almighty
and have the power to heal

Please forgive them father
they cannot be forced to believe in you
It is something they need to find in their hearts
it's something each and everyone should do

Dear father in heaven
to me it's conceivable that you are for real
Just know I believe in you
your power and blessings I can feel

Father Of Forgiveness
Continued

Each day I say prayer
to honor the blessings you give to me
Without your love dear father
I would live blindly and not be able to see

So thank you father in heaven
for the sacrifice you made out of love
When my time comes to leave this place
I am looking forward to being with you in Heaven above

E. Wayne Searles

Goodbye Dear Father

So much pain
God, why did you take him away
I am so angry inside
I can't find it within me to even pray

Feeling so broken
have no idea at the moment what to do
We needed him here more
but you took him home to be with you

I have no idea
what is your plan
I only know that today you took from us
a father, grandfather, and a wonderful man

God, we love him so much
missing him, the tears tell we do
I am so confused
about my love for you

I try to find understanding
though it is so very hard to do
Please give me a sign
my father is now there with you

I don't want to hate you
as I know he was in so much pain
I only wish you would have healed him
and gave us sunshine instead of so much rain

Goodbye Dear Father
Continued

Dear father
there is something you have to know
I know I told you many, many times
but I truly love you so

Now that you have ascended to the heavens
your pain is forever gone away
There will never be a day that I forget you
your memories are with me forever from this day

E. Wayne Searles

I've Been Astray

Sitting here at this moment
having emotions of who I have become
Having been born again as a child
my feelings now are numb

At one time I had understanding
about God and heaven above to be
Since that time I have become lost
leaving the hand of Jesus to do what I wanted for me

I have been a lost sheep
because my wonder of the world took control of me
For so many years I have been blind
once again I would like to see

Stuck here in moments of sentiment
my heart and soul cry out
I close my eyes and listen
the Christian music to which I hear, does reassure my doubt

The worldly ways in which I have lived
have brought me so much anger and pain
I don't have much more energy to go on
dear Lord forgive me for everything I have done in vain

My choices in this life
should be choices in which I can always rejoice
Just know there is a God
when you call on him, he will hear your voice

I've Been Astray
Continued

Not only should you call on him
in times of trouble or dire need
You need to give him your hand
implant his love as a seed

So at this moment I rejoice
because dear God you're always in my heart
I hold your hand in belief
knowing from this numbness I will depart

E. Wayne Searles

Message From Heaven

Eighty Eight
I would have been today
If only
the good Lord didn't take me away

It's not a bad thing
I lived a very good life
I am together again with my husband
walking the heavens as husband and wife

Toward my last days
I was in so much pain
To keep on in that world
I would have nothing to gain

I loved you all
and I still do
Even from up here in heaven
I still watch over all of you

So I am not so sad
for not reaching the age of eighty eight
The Lord had other plans for me
it was my time to enter heavens golden gate

Five months have now passed
since I left you all behind
I saw you as you wept
and heard your every word that was so kind

Message From Heaven
Continued

Just know I am in a much better place
even though I miss you all
Just know I hear you
when you miss me and my name you call

So now let me say goodbye
As for some it was too late
I will see you all when you come to heaven
I'll be waiting at heavens golden gate

E. Wayne Searles

My Belief – My Inspiration

Banned
from the fires of hell today
Because my personal beliefs
steer my soul another way

I believe in God
but do not frequent a church to pray
I can kneel down on my knees anywhere
when I have words to God to say

I don't need to be pushed
or told my ways are not right
I know my own path
and carry a torch to give me light

I do believe
there is both a heaven and a hell
But those are my beliefs
I do not drink from a different water well

I share my hand in love
my words of wisdom only when required
Knowing in God I believe
is what really keeps me so inspired

So yes my friends
I am banned from the fires of hell today
Even if you think they are just stories
and you laugh at all what I say

My Belief – My Inspiration
Continued

I only wish you well
in your journey or whatever you believe
I wish you peace and happiness
in whatever form you conceive

E. Wayne Searles

My Father's House

I stepped into his house
I felt his spirit, and I lost all fear
My soul regained energy
thoughts of repenting my sins were very sincere

The Lord knows my weaknesses
he can see the sorrow and burden in my heart
The lord knows I don't stray too far
from his family I surely will never part

I am a sinner
it just happens, getting caught up in worldly ways
Every Christian has their moments
even when Satan traps you in a faze

This world is tough
that certainly isn't a lie
Just keep your faith in Jesus
in his Holy Spirit, you can rely

I don't go to church often
but when I do, I feel the presence of Jesus our Lord
He heals me with his touch
and welcomes me aboard

He speaks through his presence
with love and warmth filling the heart
Once you give him your hand
your sense of peace and happiness will finally start

My Father's House
Continued

Jacobs Well is my home
with a family full of love that's true
It's where you can praise the Lord
and feel his spirit too

E. Wayne Searles

My Walk With God

Having been depressed
I decided to go for a walk
I listened to the nature
and with God I had a talk

I was not sure if he was listening
but I kept on sharing my pain
If anyone had seen me
they would have thought I was insane

When I was walking
I turned around and looked down
That's when I noticed
there were only one set of footprints to be found

At that moment I gasped
realizing God was carrying me
He was listening to my pain
and from it, he was trying to set me free

When I was in sorrow
depressed and lonely at a point
God carried me during that time
and with his blessings, my body he did anoint

Many people don't believe in God
everyone having their own reasons why
I have spiritual faith
my belief in God I do not deny

My Walk With God
Continued

Thank you God
for helping me through this time of need
Thank you for dying for my sins
and hanging on a cross and bleed

I am feeling much better
knowing I took a walk with God
I am a firm believer
knowing that nothing about it is so odd

E. Wayne Searles

My Friend Jesus

Nobody can see you
when you walk with me and hold my hand
People think we are crazy
and tell us all religions only cause chaos upon the land

In all my times of trouble
you are always there
You do not leave me alone
feeling sad and full of despair

When no one else will listen
you hear everything I say
When you know I am unhappy
you take my hand and say walk with me this way

Many don't believe
that you can possibly be real
They say you are only a story told
because your image, in the flesh you do not reveal

All of that does not matter to me
dear Jesus you are my friend
You stand by my side through heart ache
and give me hope when I think it's just the end

So I find myself talking to you
no myth or story to be told
I see and feel your presence
you just don't grow old

My Friend Jesus
Continued

Where should we walk today
as I am always pleased of conversations with you
I love it when you hold my hand
and tell me there is nothing I cannot do

E. Wayne Searles

Our Lord Our Father

May we give glory to God our father
and pray his son Jesus walks by our side
May the non-believers find faith
and in our heavenly father, begin to confide

These paths we walk in life
each and every day
May not always be so glorious
especially if we're not living life in Gods way

There are so many religions
many Gods in which various people do believe
I can say there is only one God over all
I just wish it is something everyone could conceive

Our father gives us life
and he also takes it away
We just don't know where and when
so daily we should pray

Not everyone believes
or wants to live the life a true Christian should live
I pray for each and every one
to our God in Heaven, your hand you give

May his angels watch over you
helping you whenever you're in need
I just pray you give your life to Jesus
for your sins he had to bleed

Our Lord Our Father
Continued

God and the son of God
more than just a story I am sure
I believe in both of them
their love is truly pure

E. Wayne Searles

The Lords Presence

I was in the house of the Lord today
the local language, I did not understand
I felt the presence of God our Lord
as if I stood there and he held my hand

The church was so big and beautiful
many sculptured relics inside and out
The church was built so many years ago
very cold inside and will echo if you scream or shout

My visit was because of Easter
I don't go to church very much
It seems I should go more often
so I can feel God's wonderful touch

As I sat there and listened
my mind often wandered so far away
Without the Lord holding my hand
I wondered how I would get through each and every day

Then I realized the answer is easy
I am a Christian, Jesus and God our father love me so
I always ask of them forgiveness
and my hand they never let go

In that church today
a real sense of peace came over me
It was once again that I realized
Heaven is a reality

The Lords Presence
Continued

Thank you dear Lord
thank you Jesus too
Thank you for all of my blessings
and for being with me in everything I do

E. Wayne Searles

The Warmth Of God

The sun is shining
I feel the rays upon my face.
It feels like passion
of God's grace.

Standing there
head tilted back.
Face feeling warm
my smile to God is not an act.

The feeling is so pleasant
I slowly fall to one knee.
A feeling of his presence
I know it is he.

The sun has power
like the touch of God's hand.
The feeling is overwhelming
enjoy it as much as you can.

As I kneel there
I hear something nearby.
It sounds like water
which makes me feel high.

With my eyes closed
I reach my hands about.
There is a touch of water
yes it's water no doubt.

The Warmth Of God
Continued

The feeling is wonderful
so much, I feel calm.
Slipping my hands in the water
picking it up with my palm.

A refreshing feeling
as I put the water on my face.
I pray to God for forgiveness
and ask for his grace.

As I open my eyes
I stand and smile towards the sun.
Squinting my eyes
I say dear Lord, my heart you have won.

E. Wayne Searles

Touched By An Angel

Touched by the wing of an angel
I heard a voice and a flutter of wings
Soft spoken words
and then a heavenly sound as the angel sings

Chosen to be my guardian
from the heavens high above
This angel presented itself to me
sharing a sentiment of love

Peace came over my body
a sense of being at its best
I know there is a heaven
where all Christians rest

The language of the angel
was in a sort of twisted tongue
But I understood every word
as I listened to the song it sung

A melody that soothed my soul
and relaxed me from all despair
I believe in angels from heaven
so this experience I need to share

Having been touched by an angel
I now see so very clear
I am ready for the next world
because my loyalty to God has been sincere

Wrong Side Of Heaven

On the wrong side of Heaven
is better off than being in Hell
I am not much for religions
but there is a God, I can tell

There has been many times
I have experienced an unknown miracle
When I tell others about it
they just laugh and get hysterical

When most people are young
religion and God makes no sense
However, when they get older
they stop their denial and defense

It is times when they are hurt
that they ask help from God
The same people that persecuted the belief
I find this very odd

However, I am not one to hate
better late than never to believe
Holding your hands out to Jesus
God's blessings you shall receive

Being true to the heart
in what you believe or what you say
Makes all the difference to God
and if he will bring you to Heaven one day

Chapter Six

Goodbye From Heaven

Many hearts have been broken
because I have left this world today
Not having a clue it would happen
not having any goodbyes to say

Confusion in everyone's mind
understanding is nowhere in sight
How could such a young life be lost
the sorrow and understanding we all fight

It only goes to show
never underestimate this life we live
It can be taken away in a second
having no goodbyes to give

My life has been taken
leaving family and friends to grieve
The Lord must have other plans for me
I hope this is something you all can conceive

So now let me say goodbye
from the heavens up above
I am in a much better place
and I send you all my love

The only thing to understand
is that life is not forever to live
It can be taken at any time
without any goodbyes to give

E. Wayne Searles

Home Town Tragedy

As I sit hear
I try and hold back my tears
I sit here and ponder
of someone else's fears

I remember my childhood
and all of the crazy things I would do
I sit here trying to fathom
the tragedy that has struck you

I may not know you
as we have never ever met
But on this day my heart bleeds
in it, pain has set

I am fortunate to have grown older
having made it through the years
I hate to see someone die so young
it's hard to hold back the tears

This is why it's so important
to show each other love every single day
Life is not guaranteed
we never know when a loved one will be taken away

Family and friends are important
communities are very important too
When tragedy hits home
everyone will be there for you

Home Town Tragedy
Continued

Life is a precious gift
at any time, the good lord can take it away
We just have to find a way to understand
and to get through each and every passing day

E. Wayne Searles

Missing You

I find you absent today
even though I still think of you
I miss yesterday
and all the things that you would do

Visions of you
are is if you are still here
I keep them in my head
because you were so dear

Oh why did you have to go
leaving me here in this place
I miss you so much
I just want to reach out and touch your face

Absent you are in the flesh
but yet you're with me every day
When I go to bed every night
I have so many things to you to say

Our time together
were so very special to me
Even when it didn't seem so
I hope that now, this you can see

Watching me from the heavens
you are with me every day too
You loved me so much
I know this to be true

Missing You
Continued

Just know I love you
I forever will
Until the day comes
when my body too becomes still

This will be a very special day
when we will reunite
I can vision it now
oh what a beautiful sight

E. Wayne Searles

Mom Left Us Today

It is with great regret
the news I bring you all today
A great woman and mother
has just passed away

My mother was the greatest
that any woman has ever been to me
She kept me under her wing
until it was time for her to flee

Bernice was a loving woman
she had so much heart and soul
She has gone to join her loved ones
up in the heavens where they will bowl

I am lost for words
I know not really what to say
I am really very sad
my mother left us all today

Rest in peace dear mother
never to be forgotten I assure
So many fond moments we shared
something I will forever endure

Rest In Peace
Bernice Gelita Searles

Written: 27 September 2015

Our Beloved Harold

Before us today was a Hero
his body we laid to rest
Harold was a husband, a father, and a mentor
he walked this earth doing everything to his best

Having served his country
this country in which he loved so dearly
He was a Veteran
putting his life on the line ever so sincerely

Harold served our community
an honored Sheriff whom we all know and love
He was a very giving man
passionate and faithful to God above

To our brother in arms
Policeman, Fire Fighter, and Veteran of WWII
You have served this country with all honor
now we all honor you

This moment of passing is sad
but the Lord reaches out his hand to you
Holding all your fond memories
is something we cherish to do

Rest in peace Harold
your work here is done
We will think of you
with each and every rising sun

IN LOVING MEMORY OF HAROLD SPIEZIO SR

E. Wayne Searles

Our Loving Doris

Deep within our hearts
we are saddened on this day
Leaving us without words
just not knowing what to say

You lived a full life
one of value at its most
Always having company over
with many stories to boast

A very hard worker
also a wonderful community volunteer
Your sweet smile and laughter
always brought other people cheer

Even though we know
life is not forever to live
The time you had with everyone
were special moments you did give

Time has now come
for you to join again with Harold in the sky
You both were wonderful people
this, nobody can deny

You will certainly be missed
your memories will always be there
Always and forever
we will have mom and pops stories to share

Our Loving Doris
Continued

Now may you rest in peace
with your beloved Pops in heaven above
We will see you in the future
but for now we all send you our precious love

In Loving Memory Of Doris Spiezio

Doris and Harold were wonderful people! Even though I traveled across the ocean and lived there, whenever I came home, I would stop in and visit them. I certainly miss those visits and laughs. May you both Rest In peace!

E. Wayne Searles

Tragedy In Nice France

Today I hand you these flowers
to show you that I care
I offer you my condolences
for your loss that is not at all fair

Not knowing how to truly express myself
I am at a big loss for words to say
However I feel the need to say I am so sorry
your loved ones have been taken away

Such a senseless and selfish act
understanding it is just so hard to do
I bow my head and pray
that the good lord will watch over all of you

Just know your loved ones
are in the heavens watching down on you today
I know it hurts so much
as you shed tears finding no words to say

The anguish and pain
is hard for anyone to take away
Just know that the world stands by your side
as we all bow our heads and pray

Dear God I say a prayer
please help everyone to find love and peace
Dear God watch over all the victims
from this tragedy taken place in Nice

Remember With A Smile

How do we get away
from the rain pouring down
When we have memories
of a lost loved one that make us frown

I assume time is the healer
that will eventually pull us away
Allowing us to see sunshine again
making memories brighter each and every day

It's very hard to lose a loved one
on any given day
It can be very hard when they're gone
leaving us with very few words to say

Getting through the tough time
is what we all must do you see
Just know that they are still there
looking down from the heavens upon you and me

When given the wings of an angel
they will be right by our side
They will help protect us
they are our guardian with their wings open wide

Letting go of them
will also set us free
No need to worry at all
as they all watch over you and me

E. Wayne Searles

So many Stairs To Heaven
A TWIN TOWERS POEM

Walking up those stairs
out of breathe and stopping for another break
Walking down the stairs
were many wounded for God sake

This morning I had a good breakfast
then I kissed the wife and kids good bye
I left the house early that morning
not knowing it was my time to die

The smoke getting thicker
every step higher it gets harder to breathe any air
Danger is calling us today
to save any lives that may be trapped there

To panic is no option
must be brave and face the fight
So many people in this building today
something is just not right

The rumbling sound begins
like an earthquake has begun
I see the light of the heavens now
much brighter than the sun

Walking up the stairs to heaven
there was no turning around
We all said our prayers
amidst that last rumbling sound

So Many Stairs To Heaven
Continued

My shield and number may be found
please bury me with dignity and pride
I will be here by Gods side watching you
and also be standing by your side

Please don't forget us
we did not know it was our time to die
We had no control over leaving you
I know you have so many questions why

Just know our hands are touching you
as we watch over you each and every day
Just know we hear you
each and every time you have something you want to say

To all our wives and children
you understood our love for our job and you
Just know we will always be by your side
when you're thinking of us, as you always do

Dedicated to all the Firemen, Firewomen, EMT's and Police Officers killed being hero's, when facing danger to save lives on September 11th, 2001

I am an author of poetry of which all poetry in my books is written by me. I enjoy writing as it passes time and helps put my mind at ease. With the way the world is today, I choose not to put too much personal information about myself in here. I am at the age of 53 and have lived a decent life so far, having traveled to many places and have met many people. I have had the honor to serve my country for eleven years in the Army and proud to say I have many Veteran Brothers and Sisters. I am from upstate New York but live abroad! I hope you have enjoyed reading my poetry. Thank you!

Feeding Our Souls Within

Poetic Quest Poetry

Author
E. Wayne Searles

FaceBook: Poetic Quest

Http://www.poetry-for-the-soul.com

How would you like to reinvent your life today?
A book about how to quickly overcome depression, anxiety and anger.

Dysfunction Interrupted
By
Audrey Sherman, PhD

www.ingramcontent.com/pod-product-compliance
Lightning Source LLC
Chambersburg PA
CBHW070556100426
42744CB00006B/304